TRAVEL L

Along T

And Other Mystical Routes

Bill McCartney

The Gray House Press
Cullman, AL, 2005

The Gray House Press 1440 Greenwood Dr. NE
Cullman, AL 35055

Printed in the United States of America

10 9 8 7 6 5 4 3 2 1

Questions regarding the ordering of this book in bulk should be sent to:

The Gray House Press
1440 Greenwood Dr. NE
Cullman, AL 35055
1.256.734.8990
bmccartney@travellighteatheavy.com

Cover photo is *Coming Rain*, Max Patch, mile marker 251.1 (4,629') 2003

Library of Congress PCN # 2005927214
McCartney, Bill
Travel Light – Eat Heavy Along the Appalachian Trail and Other Mystical Routes/Bill McCartney.
p. cm.
ISBN: 0-615-12911-0
1. Outdoor – Appalachian Trail - Food. 2. Hiking – Backpacking – Cooking.
I. Title

Recipe Submission

Submit a recipe that is included in the next edition of *Travel Light – Eat Heavy*, and your name will appear with it. You will also receive a signed edition thanking you for your recipe – absolutely free. In the event that duplicate recipes are submitted, the one with the earliest postmark will be the one considered. All ingredients must be readily available in a typical grocery store (i.e., not a specialty or ethnic store) and maintain their palatability for a trail week (fresh chicken or sushi would not be good choices). Hot meals must be prepared by adding boiling water only – no simmering, sautéing, poaching, or baking is allowed. Cold meals should be geared toward, but not limited to, quick and easy lunches.

Submit your recipes to: Travel Light Recipes, 1440 Greenwood Dr NE, Cullman, AL 35055; bmccartney@travellighteatheavy.com with "TLEH Recipe" in the Subject line, or e-mail us from www.travellighteatheavy.com.

I'm looking forward to testing your inventive recipe(s) for inclusion in the next edition!

Reader comments and suggestions on how to improve Travel Light – Eat Heavy are encouraged and should be submitted to the same address as Recipes.

To Martha
The one I had been looking for all my life
and
to my parents
Adaline and Winfred McCartney
who began my outdoor education as a wee tike.

Acknowledgments

One person may have his name on a building, bridge, or in this case a book, but nothing happens in a vacuum. This book is the result of a confluence of all of the streams filled with love and support that wash over me daily. I am grateful for family, friends, teachers, acquaintances, circumstances, other authors, and a host of other people who knowingly or unknowingly helped bring *Travel Light* to fruition.

I especially want to thank Martha, my wonderful and accomplished wife, who has been supportive through good times and bad. She really is the one I had been looking for all of my life.

I want to thank my parents, Adaline and Winfred McCartney. With every passing year, my realization of how incredibly lucky my sisters and I are to have them as parents continues to grow. They started our outdoor education early and set the stage for my life-long love affair with nature.

I also need to give a goodly dollop of thanks to Chuck Sasnette for his editing prowess. He spent many late-night hours cajoling me toward a better manuscript. Among his many talents, his wit and insights into the writing process are exceptional, and I feel extremely fortunate to count him as a friend.

Susan, one of my three wonderful sisters and the one who has a Masters in English, did the final read through. She marked where those pesky commas should be added and deleted in addition to the other fine-grained punctuation and formatting errors that needed attention.

I can assure you that any remaining rough spots, errors and omissions, or convoluted phrasing you may stumble over in this book are mine alone. I always listened to Chuck and Susan; I just didn't always have the good sense to follow their suggestions.

To the many backpackers whom I stopped on trails and in towns to ask about their food, I sincerely appreciate the kernels of wisdom you willingly shared, which have bloomed within these pages. I talked with hikers from Chili to Great Britain and lots of places in between who were always willing to stop and share what they had learned about trail food. Their (perhaps your) input flavored *Travel Light* in many positive ways.

I also want to thank the following outdoor enthusiasts for reading early drafts and offering many excellent suggestions. *Travel Light* is much better because they were willing to be part of the process.

- William Branham – Piedmont AT Hiking Club; completed the AT in 2005 after seven years of section hiking; Virginia.
- Andrea Deaton– Executive Committee Chair, Delaware Valley AMC; Pennsylvania
- Dick Doucette – Maine AT Club; Thru-hiked AT in 1996 at the tender age of 56; trail name: Mr. Bean; Maine.
- Hugh Harris – Backpacker Extraordinaire; In spite of being an accomplished attorney, he is also one of the good guys; Alabama.
- John McCrary – Manager of Hurricane Creek Park; Backpacking and climbing instructor and guide; Alabama.
- Steve Morrow – Outdoorsman Extraordinaire and Eagle Scout; "I've eaten Bill's camp food for 40 years and I'm still alive!" Tennessee.
- Alex Newmark – Board of Directors Natural Bridge AT Club; Loves Pistachios; Virginia.
- Catherine Pipan, MD – Potomac AT Club; Avid hike leader and averages being on the trail about twice a month! (I wish!); Virginia.
- Mark Stanfill, Cumberland Trail Conference; Committed to completing the Cumberland Trail, a 282 mile long "Linear State Park and State Scenic Trail;" Tennessee.

Table of Contents

Preface

One of my early camp cooking lessons occurred when I was 13 and working toward the rank of Second Class Scout. It has become known as The Great Oatmeal Debacle.

On this weekend excursion, two requirements were scheduled for completion: a) backpack all of my gear and food to camp for a minimum of one mile, and b) cook a meal for at least three people, including myself.

Thursday afternoon all of the necessary gear was neatly arranged in the bottom of my pack. In went the 10 inch sheath knife, four-cell flashlight, seven pound sleeping bag, 50 feet of 1/2 inch rope, and my shiny new hatchet.

Clothes followed: two pairs of jeans, two pairs of shorts, three shirts, and an Army surplus poncho. Just the bare essentials.

Next, Mother's kitchen was raided. An iron skillet, a three quart pot with lid, a serving spoon, a spatula, a butcher knife, a scouring pad, and a quart of dish soap were jammed into the now bulging pack.

There was no room for food. Yet, the pound of bacon, dozen eggs, loaf of bread, box of oatmeal, and pound of coffee for Saturday morning's feast had to go. Boy Scouts live by the motto, *Be Prepared*, and I was. My 50 foot hank of rope was employed to ingeniously lash the food to the pack and external frame. I was ready!

It rained. The entire world was wet and muddy and grey and leaning sideways from gale force winds as I slogged toward camp. Man against the elements! What more could a boy want!

By Saturday morning the storm front had moved on leaving us with what farmers refer to as a "soaking" rain. Following the directions in my Boy Scout Handbook, a key-hole fireplace was built and moist tender struggled successfully to turn smoke into flame. The bacon and eggs (fried in the bacon grease, yum!) were crisped. The coffee was *thick* but hot. What was to pass for "toast," was actually soggy bread with butter chunks. Yet, the most memorable part of the meal was the oatmeal.

The directions for cooking oatmeal were followed as closely as a 13 year old boy can. First: *Bring salted water to a boil and add two cups of oatmeal.* Simple. I stopped reading and started cooking, surmising one direction was enough. How hard could it be?

About 15 seconds passed before checking the oatmeal for the first time. It was definitely too runny. After discussing this unexpected occurrence with my best friend and confidant (i.e., Steve Morrow), it was determined that adding 1/2 cup would thicken it sufficiently.

Patiently waiting another 15 seconds, or so, the lid was lifted again and to our great disappointment the oatmeal was still runny. This time 3/4 cup was added.

Meanwhile, Daddy was enjoying the circus act from inside the tent. He was the Assistant Scoutmaster and believes many of Scouting's lessons are best learned through experience. As long as his charges were not in imminent danger, he rarely offered advice unless asked.

However, he had agreed to be one of the three people destined to partake and therefore, had a stake in the outcome. After the second addition of oatmeal, he casually mentioned, "Oatmeal gets a lot thicker as it cooks." And it did! In fact, it became so thick that it took both hands to pry serving size chunks out of the pot.

While the oatmeal was solidifying, the bacon and eggs had turned into cold, gelatinous blobs. The toast had lost all characteristics used to identify items that are so named. Yet, Daddy, Steve (who amazingly enough remains my best friend to this day), and I wolfed down every morsel acting as if nothing was out of the ordinary. On the drive home, I happily recorded "completed" next to the cooking and backpacking requirements in my Hand Book.

I learned two important things about camp cooking from that experience. First, it takes a Mother to remove burned-on oatmeal from a pot. Second, time spent learning about trail food (and equipment) *before* you enter the wilds is a wise investment. Every item that now enters my pack is cooked, tasted, set up, repacked, weighed, and otherwise poked, prodded, and tested before it goes in.

While many backpackers spend hours researching and testing gear to determine which items will best fit their needs, few approach food in the same way. Yet, food is what enables us to crest the next ridge and see a pair of eagles hunting over an endless expanse of green, or a Lady Slipper's perfect bloom nestled against a boulder.

I still love to cook peach cobblers, biscuits, stews and the like in a Dutch oven topped with hardwood coals. However, you will not find a single Dutch oven recipe in this book. What you will find is a much lighter and more streamlined cooking system designed specifically to meet backpackers' unique constellation of needs. It is a system that delivers light weight, nutritious and appetizing foods to keep your body satisfied mile-after-mile – with no pots to wash!

Ancient Scottish Saying

It is in the shear beauty
and purity of nature
that I find peace for my soul,
inspiration for my mind,
and love for my God

Introduction

> *I went to the woods because I wish to live deliberately, to front only the essential facts of life, and see if I could not learn what it had to teach, and not when I came to die, discover that I had not lived.*
>
> Henry David Thoreau

I love food. I love thinking about it, reading about it, shopping for it, cooking it, and most of all eating it. I also love backpacking.

So for me, honing recipes and developing menus that provide the energy required to propel us down the trail day after day has been an exciting and mouth-watering endeavor.

Travel Light – Eat Heavy was written to fill a void discovered several years ago. There was no single source that included ingredients, recipes, menus, nutritional information, and weights. The useful nuggets of information were scattered across acres of rubble.

Compiling these nuggets was a tedious and time-consuming job that someone had to do. Consequently, several years were spent collecting data by surveying hikers, scouring the internet, studying outdoor and indoor cookbooks, searching the USDA, and solicitously listening to my wife. Coupled with a past life in the restaurant business, a love of food, and a passion for backpacking, this book began taking shape.

At the end of each chapter, you will also find excerpts from the journal I kept while preparing for my first hike on the Appalachian Trail. It was a special time, and the preparation and anticipation almost as much fun as being on the trail.

Journal entries were selected as windows into my struggles, thought processes, mistakes, and successes so you can avoid stumping your toes on the same rocks that I did. For those who have already bloodied your toes, our common mistakes will affirm that you (and I) are not the only one who does such things.

The hope is that *Travel Light – Eat Heavy* will, in some small way, increase your joy in building an album of poignant memories as you travel the Green Tunnel and other mystical routes.

Six Reasons To Use This Book

> *The thinking that created the problems we face now cannot be used to solve the problems that thinking created.*
>
> Albert Einstein

Reason #1
Information is Collated For You

Unlike gear, information pertaining to the backpackers' food rubric (e.g., ingredients, meals, menus, weights) was strewn throughout a hodgepodge of sources. *Travel Light – Eat Heavy* solves that problem by collating nutritional, caloric, and weight specifications in an easy to use format. Ingredients, recipes, and menus are rendered individually and collectively, providing the precise, precalculated information you need.

To modify existing menus or recipes for your unique needs there is also an Ingredient List in the back. This list includes quantities, weights, calories, and calories/oz. to make it simple to recalculate the critical numbers.

Travel Light will quickly become an indispensable planning guide for what goes into every backpacker's food sack.

Reason #2
Your Energy on the Trail Will Increase

Too often backpackers are seen dragging into shelters, exhausted after an eight or ten mile day. Their priorities are predictable: drop the pack, treat hunger pains with carbs, and slither into their bag as the day dims. Enthusiasm for plant identification, journaling, star-gazing, and the like is often a casualty of inefficient diets.

The menus contained here provide the types and quantities of calories needed to smooth out the highs and lows that deficient diets trigger. These amalgamations will energize you all day, allowing the magic of the trail to permeate your soul – instead of fatigue driving you toward supper and sleep.

Reason #3
Your Pack Weight Will Decrease

Books and magazine articles abound on how to reduce pack weight; all share a pivotal tenet: take what you need, not need what you take.

Many of us take that advice to heart, working incessantly to jettison nonessentials. Toothbrush handles are cut off, then our half-handled ones are replaced by pet toothbrushes that slip over a finger. Excessively long pack straps are trimmed and half of us even leave our underwear at home, according to Roland Mueser (*Long-Distance Hiking*, 1998). (Next time you're on the trail don't stare, a quick glance should tell you which half he or she is in!)

The zeal for microanalyzing the "essentialness" of each gear and clothing gram, is rarely transferred to our provisions. Trail interviews and other research finds an overwhelming number of backpackers can eliminate *pounds* of unnecessary food weight and actually eat heavier.

Menus found here are based on what a male needs during a 3-season hike and average 1.8 pounds per day. For a five-day trip that equates to nine pounds, or 12.6 pounds for a week. Alternatively, women, needing fewer calories, will average 1.6 pounds per day, eight pounds for five days, or 11.2 for a week.

These weights may appear heavy to those who exist on energy bars and Pop Tarts between gorging at AYCE buffets. For those who take food sufficient to avoid hunger pains, boinking (i.e., running out of energy), or boringly repetitious meals, they represent significant reductions.

Reason #4
Home Preparation Is Easy

Increase trail time and decrease preparation time. That philosophy leads to two decisions regarding trail food. First, do not spend time slicing, dicing, peeling, and otherwise preparing dehydrated food. Second, buy everything from local grocery stores.

Preparation needs to be quick and easy. Fretting about specialty foods arriving on time and whether or not they will be what you ordered when they do arrive is not a pleasurable pastime. Equally disdainful, is the tedium of buying, preparing, dehydrating, and packaging your own ingredients. Either situation can suck the joy out of your preparation ritual.

As one alternative, some of our backpacking siblings dash to Wal-Mart for 46 energy bars, a box of Little Debbie Oatmeal Cakes, and a dozen packages of Ramen noodles. While there are significant disadvantages to inflicting a diet like that on ourselves, humans can withstand almost anything before our gag-reflex demands variation.

A more rewarding alternative is to prepare the menus found here. All ingredients are found on your grocers' shelves (except maybe the grits if you live outside of the South!). Not ordering costly ingredients or investing days in the kitchen keeps costs down both in terms of time invested and actual dollars. More importantly, the menus found here show you how to pack a delicious variety containing all the energy you will need with only a moment's notice.

Reason #5
Trail Preparation is Simple

Backpackers spend thousands of hours every year squatting on their haunches and bending over their stoves. While in this posture we also chop, measure, dump, stir, flip, drop, and burn food and fingers. A literal and figurative pain in the back results, shattering the uninitiated's visions of idyllic banquets staged among exquisite scenery.

Travel Light – Eat Heavy reintegrates pleasure into every meal. The most any recipe requires is to measure water into a pot, make it boil, and divide it between your coffee cup and a bag of dry ingredients. Within a few minutes, a piping hot meal and steaming cup of coffee are ready to be savored. When finished – all that is needed is to secure the now empty bag in a trash bag and lick your spoon … that's all folks!

Reason #6
Resupply Is Uncomplicated

Neither running out of food nor claiming your next resupply box is problematic, if they occur at the same time every time. Yet, there are those among us who relish spending an unscheduled day spread eagle in the middle of a bald with only the wind and sky to blanket them. If the latter describes you, integrating a flexible resupply system will better fit your hiking style.

No mail order, specialty, or self-dehydrated foods are found in any recipe. In fact, any grocery, in any trail town, stocks an excellent selection of backpacking food. Thus, the ability to fully resupply, whenever and wherever, is a central benefit of using *Travel Light* as a planning companion.

At home we have rigid schedules to maintain. On the trail we need to savor the freedom an evolving schedule affords. Heed the mountains' siren call as the ubiquitous Bluettes lead you to that unknown dot on earth where you will next overnight.

<u>Tuesday, May 28</u>

Having been sporadically faithful since January, I went back to the gym yesterday for the first time in three weeks. After walking on a treadmill for an hour (2.9 miles), the bottoms of my feet are a little sore. Can you imagine what it will be like to hike 8-10 hours with sweaty socks and heavy boots!? My feet must be toughened up! I am now bare footing at every opportunity.

Making Water Boil

Courage is resistance to fear, mastery of fear – not absence of fear.

Mark Twain

All Boil, No Simmer

Since time began, mountains have rewarded those hardy enough to venture into their folds with dazzling light shows as evening transitions into night. To miss even one while encumbered by a simmering pot is shameful. That is why no recipe in this book mentions the word "simmer."

"Measure water into a pot, light stove, boil water, pour" is the repetitive formula for creating the hot meals included here. Thus, the only criteria for your heat source are: 1) how quickly and efficiently it can heat water to 212° Fahrenheit, and 2) its weight.

Types Of Water-Boilers

Hikers select their personal water boiling apparatus from one of three distinct categories. I'm going to briefly explain the pros and cons of these and leave the finer distinctions to others.

Liquid fuel (e.g., gasoline, diesel, kerosene) and cartridge (i.e., butane, isopropane, propane) stoves both operate by burning pressurized fuels. Among traditional backpackers, they are the two most popular types.

<u>The Birth of Pressurized Fuel Stoves</u>

Liquid fuel and cartridge stoves both employ pressurized liquids, which in turn are vaporized, then ignited. Not surprisingly, they emanate from the same source.

Commonly used for heating and cooking in the 19th century, paraffin burners were sooty and smelly. Their eyes reddened, the masses screamed through black rimmed lips for improvement.

In chilly Stockholm, AB Separator employee, F. W. Lindqvist, heard those cries and in the late 1880s developed a solution. (AB Separator had been founded 10 years earlier, revolutionizing the milk industry with a patented cream separator.) Lindqvist's innovative contribution to public health was "a wickless pressure stove, which vaporized the paraffin before combustion and greatly reduced the amount of smoke and greatly improved the heating capacity."[1]

In 1892, Lindqvist formed a partnership with AB Separator's owner Johan Viktor Svenson. With increased production capabilities and the immediate acceptance of his "Primus" stoves, Lindqvist took advantage of rapidly expanding markets.

Norwegian Soeren Condrup bought the rights in 1893 to sell Primus stoves in the United Kingdom and North America. That same year, famous explorer, Fridtjof Nansen selected them for his expedition to Greenland. As reports of his exploits reverberated around the world, Primas achieved global renown.

Today Lindqvist's innovation continues to cook food on every trail in the world.

For more information visit: http://en.wikipedia.org/wiki/Portable_stove or www.spiritburner.com/svenson.htm.

Liquid Fuel Stoves

The liquid fuel stove was the gold standard of backpackers for years. A key to its enduring popularity is their ability to heat efficiently above 8,000' and in freezing conditions. With proper maintenance, they will provide the all the BTUs needed.

Fuel is widely available as most burn gasoline, diesel fuel, or kerosene. Collectively, the stove, fuel tank, tank-stove connector hose, and fuel will add two pounds or more to your pack weight. Performing admirably under most conditions, they are your heaviest choice.

Cartridge Stoves

Once highly problematic, cartridge stoves no longer feature leaky gaskets, inefficient fuels, slipshod production and scarce fuel. Today's better cartridge stoves rival liquid fuel stoves' efficiency, dependability, and BTU output. For ease of set-up, use, and repacking, they are superior.

While manufacturers have made great strides, canister stoves stubbornly remain less efficient in below freezing environments. Canisters are filled with liquefied gas. Opening the valve releases pressure, which permits the liquid to return to its preferred gaseous state and become ignitable.

In warm weather the liquefied gas "eagerly" returns to its gaseous state. The further the mercury drops, the less "eager" the liquid is to make the conversion thus decreasing the stove's efficiency. Adding body heat helps compensate for this shortcoming.

For instance, your canister can spend the night in your sleeping bag or ride down the trail in your coat for the last mile of the day. Even during extreme conditions, either method will heat your fuel sufficiently to boil the requisite water with little, if any, delay.

Canister fuel is now found in all well-stocked outdoor stores. If any trepidation remains about fuel availability, include a canister in your resupply boxes. I do this as a standard procedure to eliminate another stop while in town. Note – *Allow 7 to ten days for shipping as flammables must be declared and sent via ground.*

In terms of weight, canister stoves fall mid-range. Heavier than alcohol and tab stove, lighter than liquid fuel stoves.

Isopropane

Isopropane is a commonly used canister fuel. Unbeknownst to most, it also has an interesting life outside of backpacking circles.

A colorless, odorless gas, isopropane is easily liquefied and instantly returns to its gaseous state when released. These characteristics allow for its use: in disposable cigarette lighters, in the manufacturing of aviation fuels, as a calibration gas for temperature and pressure gauges, and as a propellant for hair sprays and breath fresheners.

Alcohol and Tablet Stoves

The growing cadre of ultralighters has adopted these feathery stoves, which share two commonalities. First, this category includes the lightest stoves; particularly alcohol burners, which approach weightlessness; registering a scant 2 oz. or less (not including fuel). Second, the breeze created by a herd of southbound butterflies will disturb the flame enough to turn bringing water to a boil into an endurance contest.

Alcohol stoves are often homemade from soda cans and devised in a variety of configurations. The internet offers dozens of plans, complete with illustrations. For added efficiency choose one that includes a windscreen.

Esbit (tablet) burning stoves are factory-made contrivances. They neatly fold into an orderly, square package and house their fuel cache. When hinged open, they form a fire-tablet platform, legs, and pot supports. Compared to alcohol stoves, other advantages are its solid fuel will not leak, spill, or mandate the need for repackaging unspent fuel.

Tab stoves were not new 40 years ago when I bought mine. Now rarely employed by experienced outdoor people, they continue to have an enduring niche among fresh-faced Scouts and true believers.

For an in-depth discussion about stoves, fuels, and accessories, an excellent source is *The Complete Walker IV* (Fletcher and Rawlins, 2002). It devotes 40 pages to the topic and includes more detail than you ever imagined.

Personal Stove and Fuel Consumption

To provide a basis of comparison, my current stove is a canister fueled Primus Titanium. The stove weighs 3.4 ounces including its piezo igniter, 4.5 oz. with its always used case. (A nonworking stove creates too much work. Say it with me – "Easy is good!")

This stove will produce a blowtorch like 11,000 BTUs, and will boil a cup of 40° water at 1,000' above sea level in less than two minutes. Two and a half cups of water boils in an average of four minutes, two seconds.

On average, heating two cups of water (one for the meal, and one for a hot beverage) consumes .32 oz. (8 g.) of fuel. I limit hot meals to breakfast and lunch, which results in an average fuel consumption of .64 oz. per day. The MSR IsoPro cartridge I use contains eight oz. of fuel, which equates to 25 meals, or 12.5 days of fuel. Notwithstanding these precise calculations, Murphy's Law dictates canisters be replaced every 10, not 12.5, days.

On a windy day, an aluminum foil wind screen (.2 oz.) increases any stove's efficiency 25%. Unprotected, even a light breeze will noticeably increase boil time and fuel consumption. ***Note*** *– Manufacturers do not recommend the use of wind screens with canister stoves. Heated to 120° Fahrenheit, fuel canisters become ticking bombs.*

No one, least of all me, wants to see a canister explode, whooshing flames across a dry forest floor or driving shrapnel into bodies. If you choose to use a wind screen, double check the stove-canister connection for leaks and touch the canister frequently while cooking to make sure it remains cool.

<u>Wednesday, May 29</u>

Last night the innocuous act of walking on the carpet for a few hours made my feet sensitive. The leather-soled feet of my youth are a distant memory.

I'm beginning to enjoy feeling more fit, completing 4.1 miles on a 12% grade in one hour today. The balls of my feet are more tender than yesterday; must be tougher before selecting a pebble at Springer to deposit on Katahdin.

Three more backpacking books are on their way from Amazon.com. Two are about trail/backpacking food the other is on long-distance hiking. A dehydrator needs to be built to dry jerky and other foods. Yumm!

My UPS driver delivered three more books today that I had ordered from Amazon.com. One on "advanced" backpacking and two on trail food. I was disappointed. There is more good information available about gear than can be read; yet, food information is fragmented and does not have the needed "specs." No weights, nutritional information, calorie counts, etc. It's all left for each hiker to reinvent their own wheel. Aaaaaaaaaahhhh! Frustrating.

There is a crying need for a comprehensive food book for backpackers (e.g., menus, balanced diet, tips and tricks to make meal preparation and clean-up easier, calorie counts, weights, etc.). In general, more of a prescriptive book – this is what to take, by meal, and why. One of these days maybe I'll write one.

The rubric of boot weight, materials, cost, and how cool they look has been pondered for more than two months. Woody (Sherwood), the local outfitter, and I thrashed out the merits of each facet today and a decision was made.

Woody is an interesting character. Tall, wiry, and excitable as talk turns to hiking, climbing, and kayaking. I wanted to talk about boots and he wanted to talk about a group of novices he taught to climb last weekend in North Carolina. The purpose for his conversational direction became clear when he tried to get me on the store's climbing wall. No thanks – let's get back to boots ...

Woody refocused, leveled his eyes at me, and matter-of-factly stated, "Buy a pair of Vasque Sundowners, they only weigh 2 lbs. something [actually 2 lbs. 14 oz. in size 9], and they are the boot everybody is using." High marks from BACKPACKER magazine and other sources added credence.

Momentarily torn between the new improved version at $210 and the classic version at $175; I decided the *difference is too much for a bigger padded collar and a different insole. I ordered the latter. They don't look very cool but for $35 I just won't look down.*

The Skinny on Calories

Life is a daring adventure or nothing. To keep your face toward change and behave like a free spirit in the presence of fate is strength undefeatable.

Helen Keller

Calorie confusion reigns. Although there is quality information to be gleaned from a host of sources, misconceptions and contradictions are systemically shuffled from one book or article to another.

For instance, one author says we need 3,500 calories per day, while another claims we need 6,000. Additional sources present reams of equally incongruent proclamations.

Rejecting all, I returned to the basics: discovery through personal observation. I doggedly immersed myself in seminal nutritional information and began a detailed log of everything consumed while hiking.

I am 6'1" and weigh 200 pounds. For two years I carried a 20 to 35 pound pack and hiked between 11 and 19 miles a day. Hundreds of trail miles later I learned that an average of 3,000 calories, spaced appropriately throughout the day, keeps hunger at bay and prevents boinking (i.e., running out of energy).

Records were kept during normal spring and fall AT weather. Normal in this context, includes a range from bright, 80° days to a six days deluge that turned the AT into a series of ponds connected by torrents, punctuated by electrifying light shows and five-minute temperature drops of 40°! As I have heard more than one hiker say, "The AT is all about the weather!"

Some days, 13 miles would be covered in 10 hours, while on others, 19 miles took only seven. Time and distance were contingent on terrain, weather, number of pictures taken, how many people I paused to exchange news with, and the frequency of contemplative views contemplated.

Basic Caloric Needs

As important as learning what my caloric needs are under various conditions was also determining if they are unique or applicable to other backpackers. Searching for answers, I discovered *Backpacker's Field Manual* (Curtis, 1998).

Curtis teaches outdoor skills at Princeton and over the years has developed the following guidelines.

Table 1

Caloric Needs by Season

Conditions	Calories Needed	Lbs. of Food/Day
3-Season	2,500 – 3,000	1.75 – 2.00
Cold	3,500 – 4,000	2.00 – 2.25
Winter	4,500 – 6,000	2.25 – 3.00

Source: *Backpacker's Field Manual*

Also uncovered was the FDA's (Food & Drug Administration) *Recommended Energy Intake* by sex, age, and activity, which offers a more fine-grained look. For clarity, activity levels are defined first.

Table 2

Activity Levels Defined

Activity Level	Examples
Light	Housecleaning, child care, electrical trade work, carpentry, golf, and walking on a level surface at 2.5 – 3.0 mph
Moderate	Weeding, hoeing, carrying a load, skiing, tennis, and walking at 3.5 – 4.0 mph
Heavy	Heavy manual digging, tree felling, basketball, climbing, football, and carrying a load uphill

Source: Food & Drug Administration

Table 3
Recommended Energy Intake by Sex, Age & Activity Level

Sex	Age	Light Activity	Moderate Activity	Heavy Activity
Male	19-24	2,700	3,000	3,600
	25-50	3,000	3,200	4,000
Female	19-24	2,000	2,100	2,600
	25-50	2,200	2,300	2,800

Source: Food & Drug Administration

Environmental Impacts on Caloric Needs

Experienced backpackers will realize that calculating caloric needs is not always as simple as reading a chart. Other factors, like temperature and altitude, can also exert powerful influences on energy needs. Fortunately, the U.S. Army Research Institute of Environmental Medicine (ARIEM) has a keen interest in this area too. Some of its findings are outlined below.

For a male soldier in the field (doing things like hiking and jogging with a 75 pound pack, digging fox holes, filling and stacking sandbags), the standard is 3,600 calories/day for males and 2,600 for females. These are identical to what the FDA says is needed for "Heavy Activity."

Temperature

ARIEM recommends calories be increased *up to* 4,500 calories/day for males and 3,500 for females operating in cold weather. Unfortunately, ARIEM does not make clear how cold "cold" is but, clearly, we need more energy to stay warm at -30° than we do at +30°.

Further, how many calories to add is not a linear progression. Individuals tolerate cold differently. A friend of mine wears shorts and t-shirts down to 35°, whereas, I put on a flannel shirt when the mercury plunges to 68°.

One reasoned approach to this quandary is to begin increasing calories incrementally when daily highs remain below 60° Fahrenheit. Build in 200 calorie increments (e.g., an energy bar, a Pop Tart), fine-tuning as you hone in on your body's unique requirements.

Altitude

The higher we hike the more calories we need. Unlike hiking the eons worn Appalachians, walking the spine of the Rockies or willing your self up the side of Denali places you at altitudes that require substantial caloric increases.

According to ARIEM, our caloric needs increase between 15% and 50% the higher we go. Once again, they fail to define how high "higher" is. However, experience says that at 7,000' you need to begin incrementally adding calories. A good rule of thumb is to add 200 calories at 7,000', and at every additional 1,000 feet thereafter.

<u>Rule of Thumb</u>

Our language is replete with fascinating sayings. They convey meanings that are often far removed from the actual words, yet when you just read "rule of thumb," you knew what I meant. Where did this saying come from? We cannot know for sure, but . . .

"The Oxford English Dictionary indicates that the phrase has been used for about 300 years to refer to measurements that are based on experience instead of exact science. However, some people currently believe that the phrase "rule of thumb" originated from English common law, and that the phrase reflects a law, which allowed a husband to beat his wife with a whip or stick no bigger in diameter than his thumb.

Others have used this belief as an example of feminist exaggeration. For instance, Christina Hoff Sommers, in her 1994 book <u>Who Stole Feminism: How Women have Betrayed Women</u> wrote on page 203: "Because many feminist activists and researchers have *so great a stake in exaggerating the problem and so little compunction in doing so, objective information on battery is very hard to come by . . . The 'rule of thumb' story is an example of revisionist history that feminists happily fell into believing. . . ." Jennifer J. Freyd.*

Want more? Go to: www.dynamic.uoregon.edu/~jjf/essays/ruleofthumb.html

Carbohydrates and Altitude

Metabolizing carbs requires less oxygen than fats or proteins, which makes them better suited to lower oxygen environments. At sea level air contains 20.96% oxygen; climb to 18,000' and the oxygen content per lung-full is cut in half. Therefore, the higher we hike the more efficient carbs become as calorie providers compared to fats and proteins.

Knowing this, ARIEM further recommends the percentage of calories derived from carbohydrates should be increased to as much as 60% - 70% of our total intake, the higher we hike. As with "cold" and "high," ARIEM does not define carb percentages for specific altitudes. I recommend using the same incremental approach as outlined above. Beginning at 7,000', take 200 calories from fats and proteins and add them to your carbohydrate intake. Do the same at every 1,000' increment until you dial-in your body's needs at higher elevations.

Weight's Contribution to Caloric Needs

The need to strip every possible gram from our packs fills hundreds of books and internet sites. The mantra is: Lightness reduces fatigue and increases pleasure.

A circular relationship exists between weight and amount of food needed (i.e., calories required), which bears remembering as foods are selected. An increase in food weight increases the number of calories needed to haul it, which increases the amount of food needed, which increases food weight, which increases . . . . The opposite is also true. (It is equally important to note that reducing food weight too much is also counter-productive, as explained in the following section.)

One routinely quoted factoid to illustrate the need for thoughtful weight reduction is the US Army's calculation that one pound on your feet equals 6.2 pounds in your pack. Think about it this way – your pack is static weight while you pick your feet up *thousands of times every mile.* How important is this? Let's do the math.

My average stride is 2.5', or 2,112 steps for each of the 13 miles I average per day. By reducing the weight of my footwear from 4.5 pound boots to 2.5 pound trail shoes (one pound per foot), I lift 2,112 fewer pounds every mile – an average reduction of *13 tons per day.* With a reduction of that magnitude, my body burns significantly fewer calories and I arrive at my destination fresher and ready to enjoy the evening.

Which brings us to the crux of the matter - how do pounds carried quantifiably translate into calories? Interpolate your crux using Table 4 below.

Once you have your calorie number, use it as an *estimate*, not as a definitive number. Remember that all of the factors discussed above also play a role in what *your* final number is.

Table 4

Calories Consumed During Eight Hours of Hiking and an Elevation Gain of 3,000'

Pack Weight	Body Weight			
	140#s	160#s	180#s	200#s
20#s	2,730	3,071	3,412	3,754
30#s	2,900	3,242	3,583	3,924
40#s	3,072	3,412	3,754	4,095
50#s	3,242	3,583	3,925	4,266

Source: http://www.troop609.com/pages/weightcal.html

Thru-Hikers' Needs Are Different

This book is not intended to address the needs of thru-hikers who traverse the entire trail in one gigantic bite. It is for people like me and the other 3 to 4 million people each year who only nibble at it for three weeks or less at a time.

According to The Appalachian Trail Conference, each year only 2,400 (0.0007%) out of an average 3.5 million backpackers hiking the trail attempt a thru-hike; less than 600 (0.0002%) are successful. Further reducing the likelihood that readers are thru-hikers is that section hikers, who average two to three weeks on the trail at a time, are included among the successful 600.

Thus, there is an exceedingly high probability that you are among the 99.9993% on the trail less than three weeks at a time – which definitely includes me and 3,499,999 of my best friends for whom this book is written.

Summary

The number of calories required is a highly individualized calculation involving: sex, age, temperature, altitude, body weight, pack weight, elevation gain, and a hike's duration. Metabolic rate, degree of fitness, amount of stored energy you carry around (i.e., fat), use of hiking poles, and other variables also factor into the equation.

Fortunately, like horse shoes and hand grenades, close counts here. According to Table 4, I need 3,754 calories per day while backpacking. Yet, with my metabolism, body mass index (BMI), the trails I hike, and other factors, 3,000 carefully selected and judiciously consumed calories are more than enough.

In fact, though I pack an average of 3,000 calories per day, my body is usually content with only 2,800 – 2,900. Uneaten deserts, Moose Goo, and similar items are often given away or mailed home at resupply points. The proof is in the pounds; after three weeks on the trail my weight is consistently within two pounds of when I started.

Based on personal experience and extended research, the menus offered here should satisfy the needs of most adult males. For women and younger males, there is an ingredient chart in the back to guide additions or deletions.

Types Of Calories

As important as consuming enough calories is where they originate. To illustrate, if the number of calories was the only consideration, a cup of granulated sugar provides 3,238 calories, and tips the scales at a scant 7.1 oz. Imagine, only 3.1 pounds of food for a week!

Some hikers try variations of the sugar diet, consuming hard candy and other confections when they need a boost. This short-sighted approach results in pronounced swings between vigor and lethargy as blood sugar (energy) spikes, and bottoms out, spikes, and bottoms out, spikes, and bottoms out all day.

To compound matters, a diet heavy on simple carbs (i.e., sugar) leaves blissful fullness a mere memory. Such a diet will never allow you the joy of a satisfying belch and groan to relieve the pressure. With your stomach gnawing on your backbone, life on the trail loses its allure between marathons at the AYCE buffets.

Fat-laden foods are also not the solution. Fats supply over twice as many calories per ounce than carbohydrates or protein, but a fat-filled diet is no more desirable than one too high in simple carbohydrates. Yet, fat's high caloric yield entices some ultralighters to exist almost exclusively on foods rich in fats (e.g., oils, nuts, cheese, pepperoni).

Weight as the overriding concern can eventually lead to an olive oil only diet, which has even more bang for its weight than sugar. A mere 4/10 cup weighs only 2.86 oz. and packs 3,000 calories. A week's worth of rations at only 1.25 pounds! YUM! Sip on a half cup of oil every day for a week or two – or for six months! Now that would be a memorable trip!

Thoughtful backpackers are smarter about their food and kinder to their bodies. They understand the value of tasty, filling meals to renew body and spirit. Instead of ignoring hunger pains, being well fueled allows every nerve ending to concentrate on magnificence most never comprehend as you slip quietly through the Green Tunnel.

What Are Calories?

Specifically, one calorie is the amount of energy (i.e., heat) required to raise the temperature of one gram of water one degree Celsius. So, if you could keep a Fig Newton lit, its 50 calories would release enough energy to raise the temperature of one gram of water 50° Celsius.

When discussing food, however, the term "calorie" actually refers to kilocalories, which is the amount of energy required to raise the temperature of one kilogram of water one degree Celsius. So technically a Fig Newton contains 50 kilocalories. However, we will follow the standard convention and refer to a kilocalorie as a "calorie."

In the early 1900s demand for electricity was rapidly escalating the need for greater capacity and efficiency. Steam engine generators, where small fluctuations in efficiency had little impact on profitability, were being replaced by massive steam driven turbines. Due to the increased output of these turbines, small variations in their efficiency made significant changes to the balance sheet. Yet, there was no standardized measurement to monitor or compare thermodynamic fluctuations.

Calories as an accepted measure of thermodynamic properties was already in use. The problem was they were defined in a variety of ways, which resulted in meaningless comparative information. It was like using feet, meters, cups, and pounds to compare heights.

In 1921, the American Society of Mechanical Engineers (ASME) began to pursue a standardized calorie. Germany, England, and Czechoslovakia, also recognized the problem and soon joined the American effort.

Their collaboration culminated in 1934, "with the adoption of a standard set of tables .... giving the vapor pressure as a function of temperatures, values of the column and enthalpies at points on a coarse grid of temperatures and pressures..." What emerged became the basis for a book entitled Steam Tables compiled by J. H. Keenan and G. G. Keyes. Their work became the global standard for steam powered electrical generation for the next 30 years.

And you thought calories only related to donuts . . . .

To learn more go to: www.nvl.nist.gov/pub/nistpubs/

Calorie Sources

OK, here is the obligatory introduction to carbohydrates, fats, and proteins. Included is a basic explanation of their differences and why it is important for backpackers to eat an appropriate balance. There are numerous nutrition, diet, and recipe books that are excellent and provide more in-depth information if you so desire.

Here goes . . . Carbohydrates and proteins contain approximately four calories per gram, while fats contain about nine calories per gram. The FDA uses more exact numbers, which are reflected in each recipe's nutritional information, but four and nine are close enough for most calculations.

Calories from simple carbohydrates (e.g., granulated sugar, hard candy) are processed and dumped into your blood stream almost immediately. Need a quick boost, eat some sugar. If you do, be prepared for it to also burn up quickly, creating the need to dig another "hit" out of your pocket. Commonly employed by backpackers, taking periodic hits of simple carbs has the unintentional consequence of perpetuating a miserable cycle of energy-no energy throughout the day.

Complex carbohydrates are found in foods like rice and oatmeal. They too provide energy from sugars but since they are "complex," it takes our bodies longer to separate the sugar from the rest of the food molecules. Thus, it enters your blood stream at a more leisurely pace and does not create the rapid spike and trough in energy produced by simple carbs.

Eating Oatmeal Plus for breakfast instead of a Snickers, for example, enables you to enjoy several hours of sustained energy before additional calories are needed. A Snickers may have you flying down the trail for forty-five minutes or so but your energy will soon crash, leaving you more ravenous than before.

Fat calories enter the blood stream even slower than those from complex carbohydrates, providing a longer lasting energy source. Fat is also the chief contributor to the sated feeling savored at the end of a favorite meal. Because of their high fat content, oils, nuts, salami, summer sausage, and the like are more satisfying than the same portion of a high carb, whole wheat baguette, for instance.

Trail Boosters with high fat content (e.g., cheese, Slim Jims) will power you up a long climb noticeably better than sugar. You will often enjoy a quicker recovery too.

Proteins are the least important source of energy on the trail but they are not unimportant. Your body needs protein to rebuild and add muscle as you chug up and down the endless ups and downs. Like fats, it takes time to liberate protein calories so they can migrate into the blood stream and to the muscles. Thus, they too help sustain a consistent energy level.

In sum, a fire simile provides a useful mnemonic for remembering how the three sources of calories operate.

Simple carbohydrates are like paper; they produce a hot, but short lived fire. Complex carbohydrates are like kindling, heating well but require periodic additions. Fats (and proteins to a lesser degree) are the logs, providing long-lasting heat with fewer additions needed.

Carrying the simile a little further, none of the three is sufficient to build and sustain an optimal fire by itself. We not only need some of all to fill different needs throughout the day; we need them in the right proportions.

The Right Mix of Carbs, Fats, and Proteins

From an energy needs and weight perspective, a diet containing 50% carbohydrates (primarily complex), 35% fat, and 15% protein is a good basic mix. With that distribution you will enjoy quick energy from the carbs and sustained energy from the fats and proteins.

Will you ever hit that 50-35-15 ratio exactly? Of course not. But if you use what you learn here, the results will be closer than if you just throw a jar of peanut butter, a loaf of pumpernickel, a box of Pop Tarts, and handful of bite-size Snickers left over from Halloween in your food sack.

Mother Knows Best

One bit of Motherly advice most of us have heard, "You need to eat a wide variety of food if you want to grow up to be (beautiful, big & strong, successful, or a backpacker extraordinaire)." That advice is applicable here for two important reasons.

First, eating a variety provides the vitamins and trace minerals our bodies need to sustain peak performance. Second, variety stimulates our interest in eating. If, for instance, you shudder at the idea of having to face yet another Lipton Side Dish for supper, you eat less.

You have probably read accounts of backpackers living off of GORP and energy bars for extended periods of time. While it is possible to exist on such a diet, one so limited will not provide everything your body needs as you schlep your way closer to Maine (or Georgia).

Supplements can be added to replenish what a Spartan diet does not provide – but why deprive yourself? Backpacking is supposed to be fun, not an endurance contest. Besides, how many energy bars can you swallow in a row before your gag reflex kicks in? For me it's about a day's worth.

On the other hand, if you are hiking for only a weekend, you can exist on almost anything. Forty-eight hours is not long enough for your body to shut down from nutrient deprivation or your mouth to weld itself shut when it realizes you are peeling another energy bar.

No matter what you eat on a weekend trip, there is only a slight chance of any permanent damage being done. If you eat nothing but simple carbohydrates and fats (e.g., 47 Twinkies and a can of Crisco), you can still expect to be mostly recovered by Thursday.

Thursday, May 30

I have spent months ferreting out and memorizing information on materials, production techniques, manufacturers; what features mean to quality, weight, durability, and functionality; reading trail journals; and probing the mind of every backpacker I could find. Shelves are stuffed with information that has been read, distilled, and catalogued, providing details for the essentials that fill my cranium. I've done my homework; I know what I need; I'm ready to buy.

Woody was on the climbing wall when I arrived at the outfitter's. He was sideways on all fours and crawling from left to right. (I didn't know that was possible!) He looked down, "Are you ready to be outfitted?" "Let's start with packs," I replied confidently.

In climbing togs, he led me over to his favorite brand of packs. Yanking them off the wall in rapid-fire succession, he handed them to me while describing their features. When I could no longer see over the packs stacked in my arms, continuing his narrative, he piled more at my feet. Amazingly, he did not pause to inhale until the 10th pack hit the floor.

It was my turn. I launched into an equally long-winded dissertation on my concerns about being properly fitted. My foremost concern was that my torso is 23" long and the brand of packs he was showing me did not fit torsos of that length. I referenced the short, two-inch differentiation in torso length between sizes Small and Medium; torsos "20 inches and up" were then lumped together in a "catch all" Large. As my discourse climaxed, I capped it with the only logical conclusion– my 23" torso required another brand's Extra Large, designed specifically for 22"-23" torsos.

It occurred to me that Woody had been acting a lot like Uncle Remus's Tar Baby throughout my homily, "He say nuttin' ... but he sho' did smile a lot ..." Then he said, as he whipped his measuring harness off of a nearby peg, "I think a medium is what you need but let's be sure."

Trying to harness myself in that damned thing for what seemed like forever, I wondered if the heat concentrating in my cheeks would result in spontaneous combustion. My thoughts flashed to my epitaph, "The Only Person Who Ever Actually Died From Embarrassment."

Woody finally took pity and winked, winked, then untangled me from the Chinese Puzzle. After making 13 adjustments, he walked behind me, jiggled the harness, and more to himself than to me, said, "Yep, either a medium in the top hole or a large in the bottom hole."

Digging through the pile of packs on the floor, he found the one he was looking for, jogged over to the climbing equipment; crammed two huge coils of rope into the pack, jogged back, and said, "Here, see how this medium feels." Damn! It fit like a custom made suit.

Tips and Techniques

Although no one can go back and make a brand new start, anyone can start from now and make a brand new ending.

Anonymous

You need not suffer charred fingers, squeezing food into your hat (yes, hat), and other blunders I have committed while preparing trail food. The following tips and techniques are offered for your safety, enjoyment, and consideration.

Kitchen Equipment

<u>Stove</u> – Choose the one that fits your needs, budget, and the environmental conditions in which you will be cooking. Remember, to use the system outlined here, all that is required of a stove is to boil water quickly and efficiently. For more detailed information, see the chapter titled *Making Water Boil.*

<u>Pot</u> – For solo cooking you need a pot with a minimum capacity of 3 cups and a tight fitting lid. Substitute aluminum foil for the lid to shave a little weight; use it as a coffee cup lid to keep heat in and unidentifiables out.

Dozens of practical pots are available to choose from. On opposite ends of the price and feature spectrums are MSR's $40.00 titanium kettle and Wal-Mart's $4.00 bacon grease pot. I use the former because I wanted a light weight pot with a handle and could not satisfactorily attach one to the latter.

Before investing in titanium, attempts were made to spot-weld a bracket onto a grease pot to hold a removable coat hanger handle. The design was spectacular; execution was problematic. Every attempt burned a new hole in the thin aluminum. Maybe you have a better solution!?

A pot has only two purposes in *Travel Light's* system: to contain water until it boils and to aid accurate pouring once it does. The two cited here were included because they are among the lightest (i.e., Grease Pot, 4.8 oz.; Titanium Pot 3.1 oz.).

A Brief History of Titanium

Ever wonder about titanium? Backpackers use this metal every day in ultralight applications such as: pack stays, pots, stoves, watches, knives, hiking poles, and more. It is a strong, light-weight metal routinely thought of as one of the aerospace industry's "space-age" inventions. Unbeknownst to most, it was discovered over 200 years ago in merry old England.

Titanium was first identified in 1791 by an English clergyman and amateur geologist, William Gregor, who lived in Cornwall. Presumably overcome with excitement, Gregor forgot to name his discovery. In 1795, Klaproth, a German chemist, discovered it anew and named it titanium after the Titans in Greek mythology.

Titanium is prized for its high strength, low weight, and excellent durability. While it is 60% heavier than aluminum, it is much stronger. Its strength allows thinner components, thereby, less weighty products. The thinness of a titanium pot's walls, for instance, makes it lighter than an aluminum equivalent.

Used in exotic applications like replacement parts for humans' bones and joints, titanium is also employed in a plethora of commercial applications. Yet, its principal commercial appeal is as a whitener in paint, paper, and food coloring. That's right, your hiking poles could have become the whitener for this page!

For more enlightenment, see:www.river citybikes.com, www.webelements.com, or www.itponline.com

Cozie Hat – A watch-cap style hat is required in this system to insulate meals while they cook, with fleece a better choice than knitted. The latter allows more heat loss during the cooking process, particularly if it is breezy.

The vast majority of hikes occur spring through fall when one hat is ample. For those who enjoy winter hikes, use two hats; one as base and the other as a top layer.

A word of caution: *Declare your cooking hat a kitchen item only. Food will drip on it, and odors will permeate it, which are excellent attractants for fur-bearing quadrupeds.*

If you need further encouragement, think about how difficult it would be to sleep while a bear chews on a hat that contains your head. To a somewhat lesser degree, inviting shelter mice, skunks, and raccoons to snack on your hair at 3:00 a.m. is equally entertaining for your shelter mates.

Keep your cooking hat with your food; don't ever wear it; hang your food bag at least 15' off the ground – every night.

Cup – This ancient device will be used for drinking, dipping out of seeps, and measuring water for meals. Titanium, aluminum, or plastic; handled or lidded are features to consider.

A favorite is the cheap, usually green, plastic coffee cup that comes with mess kits. They are also occasionally offered individually on Campmor's and other web sites. This ubiquitous 8 oz. cup has ¼ cup graduations, weighs only .6 oz., is durable, and has a handle. Its major negative is no lid. Even so, if you use an aluminum foil lid for your pot (see Pot above) this negative is easily negated.

Eating Utensil – There is a myriad of utensils that will shovel food into your mouth. The stainless steel knife-fork-spoon set that have been sold by the millions is a good choice when weight is inconsequential. Backpackers however, tend to pare their eating tools down to either a spork or spoon.

Sporks (combination spoon and fork) range from expensive titanium to free plastic ones that accompany buckets of fried chicken. Unfortunately, spork's attempt at schizophrenic utility retards both functions.

Many backpackers opt for mundane spoons. Plastic ones are free from the same fried chicken vendor dispensing sporks and from other fast food outlets. More durable ones of stainless steel or lexan are found at outfitters and discount stores. I have been using a lexan spoon with a shortened handle for three years; when it is finally lost, a twin will replace it. It weighs .2 oz., has been indestructible, and does not come with an instruction manual.

Selecting your food shoveler is limited to two overriding considerations: 1) it needs to be durable enough to last the entire trip, and 2) the handle should be long enough for the business end to reach the bottom of a quart zip bag. (The latter is particularly important when desserting on pudding or cheesecake.) For some, a third important consideration is weight, but how heavy can a heavy spoon possibly be?

Squeeze Tube – There are several references to squeeze tubes in *Travel Light's* recipes. They are like giant, refillable toothpaste tubes and can be found in discount and outdoor stores. The bottom opens for easy filling and washing, and each tube holds a scant cup. However, the plastic-slid-on-clip-cylinder-closure-device is maddening and breaks easily. If you use these tubes, buy extra clips.

An alternative to squeeze tubes is a zip bag. If you have one portion in a bag, they can be used like a chef's pastry bag. Twist and squeeze the bag until the contents are trapped in a bottom corner. Then cut the corner off and squeeze the ingredients out.

The contents could also be spooned out if you don't mind getting it on your fingers and hand. Although, it is much more fun to pretend that you are a famous French pastry chef as you ribbon designs onto your pita.

Wind Screen – Purchased or made, some completely encircle the stove while others have an opening for easier access to flame adjustments and your pot. Either style effectively protects the flame, conserving heat and fuel.

My choice is to origami one from aluminum foil. It is cheap, light, and can be instantly customized to completely encircle or not. If you prefer, pre-fabricated ones are available on-line and from local outfitters.

Regardless of style, windscreens are helpful when convection currents waft softly through the shade. They are indispensable when a weather front turns those air currents into atmospheric torrents crashing through the trees. **Warning** – *Canister stove manufacturers warn against using wind screens with their stoves.*

At Home

Write It Down – Using a permanent marker, write on each meal's bag: the meal's name, amount of water needed, and cooking time *before* the ingredients go in. Writing over noodles, nuts, and other lumpy ingredients makes it needlessly difficult.

Measure Every Ingredient – Guesstimating usually results in larger portions than needed. We cannot help it – the mantra, "I would rather have a little more than not enough," is ingrained from living with so much abundance. We *need* that little extra for our psychological, not physical, security. So, like Linus's blanket, we take pounds of extra food (and gear), which are destined to be returned to our pantries or given away. I am not suggesting you live a Spartan trail life, only that you take what is needed - not need what you take.

Zipper Bags – Storage bags are sufficiently strong to store and cook meals and are half the weight of freezer bags. The only caveat is meals that include Chinese noodles or other ingredients with sharp points. Sharp points are less likely to perforate a freezer bag's thicker plastic while grinding around in your pack.

Sandwich bags, on the other hand, should never be used to cook in. The zippers are not strong enough to prevent blow outs when mixing (i.e., kneading) water and ingredients. However, they are half the weight of storage bags, making them the better choice to segregate ingredients.

For example, when packaging the Cherry Cheesecake dessert, the Graham Crackers should be packaged separately in a sandwich bag. They are particularly susceptible to moisture; even the small amounts contained in the accompanying "dried" cherries will make Graham Crackers lose their crispness.

Package Complete Meals – Package everything needed for a meal in a "master bag." For instance, after measuring the Oatmeal Plus ingredients into its zip bag, an individually wrapped coffee bag is added. In the dim light of a birthing day, only one bag has to be located, and your meal and morning beverage are in hand.

When packaging suppers, accompanying beverages and desserts are likewise included. The use of this routine makes your life on the trail easier. Say it with me – "Easy is good!"

Package Meals By Category – It is helpful beyond belief to have your food divided among four one-gallon bags: one each for breakfasts, lunches, suppers, and trail boosters (i.e., snacks). Because of their bulk a fifth bag may be needed for pitas and tortillas.

This simple organizational tool prevents jumbled food, uncorked tempers, and meal time hassles. Instead, it will nurture " . . . that peaceful, easy feelin' . . ." Sing it with me . . .

Packaging Olive Oil – To package olive oil or other messy liquids, use a light-weight squeeze bottle with a push-pull closure. They are inexpensive, leaks are rare, and the ones I use hold about 6 oz., which is ideal for five to seven day resupply schedules.

A simple trick to prevent oiling everything in your food sack is to lick the bottle's closure after each use. A drop of olive oil here and a drop there will coat *everything*.

These handy little bottles are available in discount and drug stores, usually in Health and Beauty Aids. They also come in different colors to cue quick identification of contents.

Preparing and Eating Meals on the Trail

Measuring Water - Measure water before, not after, it boils. It is much easier, you are less likely to get burned, and you will boil only the amount of water you need, no more, no less.

Let's say you are having Creamy Craisin Nuts (CCN) and a cup of coffee for breakfast. CCN requires 1 1/4 cups of water; coffee needs 1 cup. So, using your coffee cup, measure 2 1/4 cups of water into your pot and light the stove. When the water boils, fill your coffee cup *first*. Empty the remaining water into the CCN; amazingly, it will be precisely the 1 1/4 cups needed!

Conserve Fuel – Be vigilant. As soon as your water reaches a boil, turn the stove off. Fill your coffee cup first (if having a hot beverage) then cover it with your pot's lid to hold the heat in. The remaining water is then poured into the opened food bag nestled in your cooking hat.

The bag and hat are rolled to seal in the heat and to cook your meal.

> A Cautionary Tale: *One evening, at the end of a particularly strenuous day of ups and downs, I entered a fatigue-induced stupor. After filling my coffee cup with boiling water, I placed a naked food bag in my left hand.*
>
> *With the pot of boiling water poised in my right hand, I entertained a fleeting thought about the water being exceedingly hot, which would cause my palm's uninsulated nerve endings to painfully scream, "STOP! The water is 212° and cooking your flesh!" As quickly as it flashed, I discounted it.*
>
> *In my muddled state, I decided the food in the bag would insulate my hand sufficiently, thereby eliminating the risk. I confidently poured the water in.*
>
> *Instantaneously, and of their own volition, my throat accompanied the afore mentioned nerve endings to create a duet of screams that my shelter mates later said was somewhat startling … followed by a vocabulary dump that children and grandmothers should not be exposed to.*
>
> *The take-away from this anecdote: No matter how tired you are or what else is on your mind, always put the bag in your cozie hat before adding the boiling water.*

Squeeze Out The Air – After adding water, squeeze the air out of your food bag and seal it completely. I repeat – seal the bag completely. Food that oozes into your hat as you knead the bag is not easy to clean up and even more difficult to eat. Eliminating the air allows expansion room for the steam trapped inside the bag, which helps prevent blow-outs.

Form an Insulated Bowl – After the meal has cooked the prescribed amount of time, roll the open end of the hat down to form an insulated bowl. If you are using a stubby spoon, squeeze the food up from the bottom to make reaching those last few morsels less messy.

Lick Your Spoon – Lick your spoon and add the empty meal bag(s) to your garbage bag. Treat everyone within ear shot to a full-throated belch to announce the end of another fine meal and you're done!

Wednesday, June 5

I can now walk a 7% grade for an hour at 3.7 mph on the treadmill. Millions of superfluous calories are being burned off – the ol' body is closer to ready!

The bottoms of my feet didn't feel tender after finishing my workout. Two weeks of going barefoot while walking the dogs, and my "road work" at the gym are paying off.

Woody called to tell me my boots had arrived yesterday morning. They weighed in at 4 lbs. 1 oz., which is a long way from the advertised 2 lbs. 13 oz. Only two shoe sizes larger than the boots in the specs but 44% heavier! In spite of the disappointing weight, they are still one of the best options.

With almost two days of break-in, the boots are beginning to feel comfortable. The only exception is where they rub the outside of both ankles. I'll have to limber up and expand the leather with a pocket knife. (Rubbing and pushing vigorously with the end of the knife's handle, not the blade!)

Menus That Will Keep You Going

Each soul must meet the morning sun, the new, sweet earth, and the Great Silence alone!
Ohiyesa (Dr. Charles A. Eastman)

When every meal begins to look and taste the same, we lose interest, our appetites diminish, so we eat less. The Army calls this "ration monotony," which it identified as causing a spiraling degradation of soldiers' caloric intake and performance capabilities. It is so critical to performance that the military spends millions of dollars every year to prevent it. Backpackers should also be mindful of this barrier to optimum performance.

This chapter contains menus for two weeks, that are designed to prevent ration monotony from rearing its ugly head and spoiling an otherwise excellent adventure. Hot, cold, Italian, Mexican, Chinese, and more are included to provide a delicious variety. All sensory experiences on the trail should be relished, including your meals.

Menus are calculated to provide an average of 3,000 calories per day derived from: 50% carbohydrates, 37% fats, and 13% proteins. They provide the mix of energy sources, in the quantities needed, to fuel adult males all day. Women should use the information in Appendix A to reduce their menus to an average of 2,100 calories per day and to lighten their loads.

If you are going to be backpacking for only a few days, select daily menus you will enjoy the most or ones for which you already have the ingredients in your pantry. For long escapades, eat your way from day one to day 14, then repeat the cycle. Two weeks is enough spacing to avoid ration monotony no matter how long you are on the trail.

For the gram-weenies among us, the average food weight per day is 802.3 g., 28.3 oz., or 1.8 pounds. Can your food weight be reduced further? Not if you want to maintain a tasty diet that provides the types and quantities of calories you need to feel good and enjoy every day to the fullest.

Have Your Recipes Included In The Second Edition

If you submit a recipe that is included in the next edition of *Travel Light – Eat Heavy*, you will be named as the contributor. You will also receive a signed edition – absolutely free. In the event that duplicate recipes are submitted, the one with the earliest postmark will be the one considered.

All ingredients must be readily available in a typical grocery store (i.e., not a specialty or ethnic store) and maintain their palatability for a trail week (fresh chicken or sushi would not be good choices). Hot meals must be prepared by adding boiling water only – no simmering, sautéing, poaching, or baking is allowed. Cold meals should be geared toward, but not limited to, quick and easy lunches.

Submit your recipes to bmccartney@travellighteatheavy.com and type "TLEH Recipe" in the subject line. I'm looking forward to testing your inventive recipe(s) for inclusion in the next edition!

Daily Menus

Recipes, weights, caloric, and nutritional information are located on the pages in parentheses. In the chapter on Trail Boosters (i.e., snacks) each group of snacks is designated with a number (e.g., Trail Booster #1, Trail Booster #2).. Those numbers correspond to the day's menu in which it is found. Thus, Trail Boosters #1 is included in Day One's specs (calorie count, weight, and nutritional information), Trail Booster #2 is included in Day Two's specs, etc.

Day One

Trail Boosters	1 Harvest Bar, 2 Pop Tarts, 2 Slim Jims (p. 109)
Breakfast	Regularity (p. 44)
Lunch	Mediterranean Moose (p. 67)
Supper	Rice Jerky (p. 88)
Dessert	Brownie (p. 94)

Totals

2,658 Calories; Calories From Carbs 59%; Fats 31%, Protein, 10%; Weight: 29.4 oz., 1.8 pounds.

Day Two

Trail Boosters	1 Harvest Bar, 1/2 c. Circa 1963 GORP, Power Bar (p. 109)
Breakfast	Quick Oatmeal Plus (p. 55)
Lunch	Chick 'n Pot Pita (p. 64)
Supper	Mexican Rice (p. 85)
Dessert	Snickers (p. 104)

Totals

Calories 2,906; Calories From Carbs 57%, Fats 29%, Protein, 14%; Weight 31.5 oz., 2.0 pounds.

Day Three

Trail Boosters	2 oz. Cheddar Cheese, 1/4 c. Sunflower Seeds, 1/4 c. Cashews, 1 Cliff Bar (p. 110)
Breakfast	Gritty Nuts & Raisins (p. 50)
Lunch	Bagel & Moose (p. 62)
Supper	Curried Cashew Rice (p. 78)
Dessert	Rocky Road (p. 102)

Totals

Calories 3,346; Calories From Carbs, 43%, Fats 43%, Protein, 14%; Weight 31.6 oz., 2.0 pounds

Day Four

Trail Boosters	2 Pop Tarts, 1 Harvest Bar, 2 Slim Jims (p. 110)
Breakfast	Golden Sesame BBs (p. 49)
Lunch	Sausage Nuts Walking (p. 71)

Supper	Golden Brown Rice (p. 82)
Dessert	Chocolate Vanilla Pudding (p. 98)

Totals

Calories 3,253 calories, Calories From Carbs, 56%, Fats 34%, Protein, 10%; Weight: 29.1 oz., 1.8 pounds

Day Five

Trail Boosters	1/4 c. Sunflower Seeds, 1/4 c. Cashews, 2 Harvest Bars (p. 111)
Breakfast	Bulgur Breakfast (p. 47)
Lunch	Mexican-Italian Roll Ups (p. 69)
Supper	Potato Bacon Soup (p. 86)
Dessert	Nutella Roll Up (p. 100)

Totals

Calories: 3,178 calories, Calories From Carbs, 51%, Fats 36%, Protein, 13%; Weight: 28.1 oz., 1.8 pounds

Day Six

Trail Boosters	1 Snickers, 1 Pria Bar, 2 Slim Jims (p. 111)
Breakfast	Breakfast Burrito (p. 46)
Lunch	Spam Sandwich (p. 72)
Supper	Meat & Taters (p. 84)
Dessert	Fig Newtons (p. 99)

Totals

Calories: 2,584 calories, Calories From Carbs, 43%, Fats 41%, Protein, 16%; Weight 26.8 oz., 1.7 pounds

Day Seven

Trail Boosters	1 Snickers, 1 Power Bar, 2 Slim Jims (p. 111)
Breakfast	Hang Dog (p. 51)
Lunch	Mediterranean Pepperoni & Beans (p. 67)
Supper	Chicken Nuts & Rice (p. 74)
Dessert	Oreo Pudding (p. 100)

Totals

Calories: 3,301 calories, Calories From Carbs, 52%, Fats 36%, Protein, 12%; Weight 36.1 oz., 2.25 pounds

Day Eight

Trail Boosters	1 Power Bar, 1 oz. Cheddar Cheese, 2 Pop Tarts (p. 112)
Breakfast	Beaver Nuts & Cherries (p. 45)
Lunch	Mediterranean Calzone (p. 66)
Supper	Three Cheese Tortellini (p. 90)
Dessert	Homesteader's Delight (p. 99)

<u>Totals</u>
Calories: 2,718 calories; Calories From Carbs, 49%, Fats 39%, Protein, 12%; Weight 24.6 oz., 1.5 pounds

Day Nine

Trail Boosters	1 Cliff Bar, 1 bag M&M Peanuts, 2 Slim Jims (p. 112)
Breakfast	Creamy Craisin Nuts (p. 48)
Lunch	Sausage Tortilla Roll Ups (p. 72)
Supper	Garlicky Shrimp Alfredo (p. 79)
Dessert	Rice Crispy Treat (p. 101)

<u>Totals</u>
Calories: 2,847 calories; Calories From Carbs, 46%, Fats 38%, Protein, 16%; Weight: 29.3 oz., 1.8 pounds

Day Ten

Trail Boosters	1 Cliff Bar, 2 oz. Cheddar Cheese, 2 Slim Jims (p. 113)
Breakfast	Tart Smoothie (p. 58)
Lunch	Mexican Fiesta (p. 68)
Supper	Crabby Alfredo (p. 77)
Dessert	Yogurt Covered Raisins (p. 104)

<u>Totals</u>
Calories: 2,820 calories; Calories From Carbs, 52%, Fats 32%, Protein, 16%; Weight 32.5 oz., 2.0 pounds

Day Eleven

Trail Boosters	1 bag M&M Peanuts, 1 oz. Cheddar Cheese, 1/2 c. Granola (p. 113)
Breakfast	Instant Breakfast (p. 53)
Lunch	Mediterranean BCT (p. 65)

Supper	Sausage Pot (p. 89)
Dessert	Cheese Danish (p. 95)

Totals

Calories: 2,904 calories; Calories From Carbs, 44%, Fats 41%, Protein, 15%; Weight 27.0 oz., 1.7 pounds

Day Twelve

Trail Boosters	1/2 c. Granola, 2 oz. Cheddar Cheese, 1 bag M&M Plain (p. 113)
Breakfast	Rice Cherries (p. 56)
Lunch	Bean & Bacon Burrito (p. 63)
Supper	General Athike (p. 81)
Dessert	Rice Pudding (p. 106)

Totals

Calories: 3,179 calories: Calories From Carbs, 50%, Fats 35%, Protein, 15%; Weight 29.6 oz., 1.9 pounds

Day Thirteen

Trail Boosters	1/4 c. Apricots, 1/4 c. Banana Chips, 1/3 c. Pistachios, 1 Marathon Bar, 1 oz. Cheddar Cheese (p. 114)
Breakfast	Southern Cous (p. 57)
Lunch	Bacon, Cheese & Tomato Roll Up (p. 61)
Supper	Tofu Miso (p. 91)
Dessert	Chocolate Mocha Pudding (p. 97)

Totals

Calories: 2,977 calories; Calories From Carbs, 45%, Fats 42%, Protein, 13%; Weight: 27.2 oz., 1.7 pounds

Day Fourteen

Trail Boosters	1/4 c. Walnuts, 1/4 c. Cashews, 2 Pop Tarts (p. 114)
Breakfast	Oatmeal Plus (p. 54)
Lunch	Pocket Pizza (p. 70)
Supper	Chicken Tetrazini (p. 76)
Dessert	Cherry Cheesecake (p. 96)

Totals

Calories: 3,489; Calories From Carbs, 48%, Fats 39%, Protein, 13%; Weight: 28.3 oz., 1.8 pounds

Averages Per Day

Calories: 2,994, Calories From Carbs, 50%, Fats 37%, Protein, 13%; Weight: 29.5 oz., 1.8 pounds

Saturday, June 8

A common malady among hikers, particularly males, is rubbing the skin off of body parts ensconced in their underwear. Repeatedly swinging your legs back and forth against sweaty underwear has a particularly chaffing effect. An appreciation for why 60% of male backpackers do not wear underwear is coming into focus.

I have not yet suffered sufficiently to give up the security underwear provides – new fabrics and styles are being tested. Silk boxers were worn to the gym yesterday. Bad move. Although silk feels light and smooth when dry, it turns into a vicious, sandpaper-like material when soaked with sweat.

On-line outfitters were hunted down today and three pairs of underwear were ordered (why is one underwear a pair?). All are made of unnatural fabrics and all purport to be a miracle waiting to happen in my pants. I can't wait ...

Better news on the sock front. Each new pair was worn for a day, then rated from 1 to 10 on my highly subjective, pseudo-scientific scale. The Smartwool Hiking Socks for $15.95 earned a 6; the REI Merino Wool Hiking Sock for $9.00 was awarded a 7 ½; the Thorlo Hiker Wool/Thor•lon with mid-weight padding for $11.50 took top honors with a whopping 9! It would have received a 10 but room needed to be left at the top in case something better emerges.

Diligent pack weight reductions have been rewarded with a current pack weight of a hair over 25 pounds. Having a pack five pounds lighter is exciting, given the limitations of 13 ½ pounds of basics: pack, sleeping bag, tent, and sleeping pad. How exciting? I'll know after a few climbs.

Breakfast

If you fall and break your legs, don't come running to me.

Samuel Goldwyn

Your Mother is still right. "Breakfast," a derivative of "break your overnight fast," is the most important meal of the day. Our food stores are depleted after fasting for eight to 10 hours and need to be restocked. With the amount of energy backpackers begin expending soon after waking, breakfast is of particular importance.

Included breakfasts are both hot and cold. Some are designed to be eaten in sheltered comfort. Others are to be munched as you ease along that deeply worn furrow, shivering with anticipation as the sky begins its familiar transition from black to gray. All provide the fuel you need to sashay for hours.

Health Note - *The first few days on the trail place new stresses on our body's systems. One of the ways our body retaliates for this sudden increase in demands on it is through constipation.*

Factors contributing to our rectal rebellions are: becoming dehydrated, introducing a diet low in fiber and high in fat and sugars, and increased physical stress.

When your system is inadequately hydrated, your body "chooses" between routing water to sweat glands for cooling, or to your bowels to aid the elimination process. Between sweat and elimination, the latter is short changed because overheating will kill you quicker than being constipated. Without the needed water, stools become hard, dry, and more difficult for the colon to push along.

Fiber's role in elimination is to provide bulk for easier stool formation; it also speeds the stool through the colon. Backpackers should include high fiber foods, such as bran, fruit, nuts, seeds, and beans in their daily diets. The Cleveland Clinic and National Institutes of Health (NIH) recommend 20 – 25 grams of fiber per day. Regularity (breakfast found below) provides over 60% (13.8 g) of the recommended amount.

If constipation is a consistent problem, eat Regularity for two or three breakfasts in a row and concentrate on staying well hydrated. If you need more help, boost your fiber intake by substituting Bran Buds for the Grape Nuts. At the same time, drink enough water to force frequent stops and keep your urine clear. Dark urine indicates the need to increase your fluid intake.

If you remain constipated longer than four days, many experts recommend an immediate visit to a doctor. It is a condition that creates some nasty health problems if not resolved.

To learn more, visit:
http://digestive.niddk.nih.gov/ddiseases/pubs/constipation/

Regularity

1	cup	Grape Nuts
1/3	cup	Instant Nonfat Dehydrated Milk
1/2	cup	Dried Apples
1 1/2	cup	Water

Weight, 7.7 oz.|Cook, 3 minutes|Calories, 530

At Home

Using a permanent marker, write on a quart storage bag: the meal's name, amount of water needed, and cooking time. Now, place all of the dry ingredients in the bag.

If you want the Grape Nuts to stay crisp, segregate the apples in a sandwich bag so the cereal won't absorb their moisture. Either way, the apples are added to the quart bag.

Preparation

Measure the water into your pot and begin heating. Place the opened bag into your cooking hat. When the water boils, pinch one side of its "zipper" to hold it open while pouring the water in slowly. Press most of the air out of the bag and seal completely.

Tuck the bag into the hat and roll them together to prevent heat loss. Knead vigorously enough to mix the ingredients but not so hard as to pop the bag open.

When cooked, roll the hat down to form an insulated bowl and enjoy.

Nutrition Facts

Nutrition: 530.0 calories; 3% calories from fat; 2.4g total fat; 0.5 mg cholesterol; 763.1 mg sodium; 594.5mg potassium; 123.9g carbohydrates; 13.8g fiber; 39.8g sugar; 13.8g protein.

Note

Works equally well as a cold cereal if you do not want to take the time to boil the water.

Beaver Nuts & Cherries

1/2	cup	Couscous
1/4	cup	Dried Cherries
1/4	cup	Walnuts
1	pinch	Salt
1/2	cup	Water

Weight, 5.5 oz. | Cook, 5 minutes | Calories, 636

At Home

Using a permanent marker, write on a quart storage bag: the meal's name, amount of water needed, and cooking time. Now, place all dry ingredients in the bag.

Preparation

Measure the water into your pot and begin heating. Place the opened bag into your cooking hat. When the water boils, pinch one side of its "zipper" to hold it open while pouring the water in slowly. Press most of the air out of the bag and seal completely.

Tuck the bag into the hat and roll them together to prevent heat loss. Knead vigorously enough to mix the ingredients but not so hard as to pop the bag open.

Cooking

Let your meal cook in the hat for 5 minutes with no peeking. Remix (i.e., knead) twice more while cooking to ensure even distribution of water and ingredients.

When cooked, roll down the top of the hat to form an insulated bowl and enjoy.

Nutrition Facts

Nutrition: 636.5 calories; 26% calories from fat; 20.1g total fat; 0.0mg cholesterol; 307.3mg sodium; 272.6mg potassium; 101.0g carbohydrates; 8.3g fiber; 0.8g sugar; 16.5g protein.

Breakfast Burritos

2		Flour Tortillas, 6 inch
1/2	cup	Refried Beans (p. 124)
2	oz.	Cheddar Cheese
2	tbsp.	Real Bacon Bits

Weight, 7.1 oz. | Cook, 0 minutes | Calories, 606

At Home

Using a permanent marker, write on a quart storage bag: the meal's name, amount of water needed, and cooking time. Now place the bacon bits and individually wrapped cheese sticks (or plastic wrapped chunk) in the bag.

The tortillas should remain in their original packaging or be placed in a separate bag. The beans should be packaged in a squeeze tube or something similar.

At Meal Time

Spread half of the beans on each tortilla. Sprinkle half of the bacon bits and add a cheese stick to the beds of beans. Roll to form two burritos and enjoy.

Nutrition Facts

Nutrition: 606.6 calories; 46% calories from fat; 55.3g total fat; 79.6mg cholesterol; 1635.9mg sodium; 491.2mg potassium; 53.2g carbohydrates; 8.7g fiber; 1.8g sugar; 32.3g protein.

Bulgur Breakfast

1/2	cup	Bulgur
1/3	cup	Craisins
1/4	cup	Walnuts
2	tbsp.	Brown Sugar
1	pinch	Salt
1	cup	Water

Weight, 6.3 oz.|Cook, Overnight|Calories, 659

At Home

Using a permanent marker, write on a quart storage bag: the meal's name, amount of water needed, and cooking time. Now place all of the dry ingredients, except the walnuts, in it.

Place the walnuts in a sandwich bag, roll it and insert in first bag.

The walnuts can be used straight out of the bag or can. However, toasting them for a few minutes in a cake pan at 350° until lightly browned will give them a much more deliciously pronounced flavor.

Preparation The Night Before

Using cold water, measure out the amount needed. Take the bag of walnuts out and set aside. Open the bulgur bag and pinch one side of its "zipper" to hold it open, then pour the water in slowly. Press most of the air out of the bag and seal completely. Knead the ingredients to *thoroughly mix*, then return it to your food sack, along with the walnut bag. Hang your food sack for the night.

The Next Morning

Add the walnuts, reseal the bag and knead to mix them throughout.

When mixed, fold down the top of the hat to form a comfortable bowl and enjoy.

Nutrition Facts

Nutrition: 658.8 calories; 26% calories from fat; 20.6g total fat; 0.0mg cholesterol; 319.8mg sodium; 527.4mg potassium; 117.2g carbohydrates; 17.1g fiber; 53.8g sugar; 13.1g protein.

Creamy Craisin Nuts

1/2	cup	Instant Cream of Wheat
1/4	cup	Craisins (Dried Cranberries)
1/4	cup	Walnut Pieces
2	tbsp.	Brown Sugar
1/2	tsp.	Cinnamon
1	pinch	Salt
1 1/4	cups	Water

Weight, 6.3 oz. | Cook, 5 minutes | Calories, 717

At Home

Using a permanent marker, write on a quart storage bag: the meal's name, amount of water needed, and cooking time. Now place all dry ingredients in the bag.

Preparation

Measure the water into your pot and begin heating. Place the opened bag in your cooking hat. When the water boils, pinch one side of its "zipper" to hold it open while pouring the water in slowly. Press most of the air out of the bag and seal completely.

Tuck the bag into the hat and roll them together to prevent heat loss. Knead vigorously enough to mix the ingredients but not so hard as to pop the bag open.

Cooking

Let your meal cook in the hat for 5 minutes without peeking. Remix (i.e., knead) twice more during cooking time to ensure even distribution of water and ingredients.

When cooked, roll down the hat to form an insulated bowl and enjoy.

Nutrition Facts

Nutrition: 717.0 calories; 24% calories from fat; 20.8g total fat; 0.0mg cholesterol; 322.5mg sodium; 344.4mg potassium; 123.8g carbohydrates; 7.2g fiber; 47.3g sugar; 14.0g protein.

Golden Sesame BBs

1/2	cup	Couscous
1/4	cup	Golden Raisins
3	tbsp.	Sesame Seed
1/8	cup	Brown Sugar (2 tbsp.)
1	pinch	Salt
1/2	cup	Water

Weight, 6.0 oz.|Cook, 4 minutes|Calories, 693

At Home

Using a permanent marker, write on a quart storage bag: the meal's name, amount of water needed, and cooking time. Now, place all of the dry ingredients, except the sesame seeds, in it. Measure the sesame seeds into a sandwich bag, roll it up, and place inside the quart bag.

The sesame seeds can be used as purchased. However, toasting them for a few minutes in a cake pan at 350° until lightly browned will give them a more pronounced flavor.

Preparation

Measure the water into your pot and begin heating. Place the opened bag into your cooking hat; remove the sesame seeds and set them aside. When the water boils, pinch one side of its "zipper" to hold it open while pouring the water in slowly. Press most of the air out of the bag and seal completely.

Tuck the bag into the hat and roll them together to prevent heat loss. Knead vigorously enough to mix the ingredients but not so hard as to pop the bag open.

Cooking

Let your BBs cook in the hat for 4 minutes without peeking. Remix (i.e., knead) twice more during cooking time to ensure even distribution of water and ingredients.

Before Eating

Add the sesame seeds, reseal the bag, and knead to mix them throughout.

When cooked, roll down the top of the hat to form an insulated bowl and enjoy.

Nutrition Facts

Nutrition: 693.1 calories; 17% calories from fat; 14.1g total fat; 0.0mg cholesterol; 319.8mg sodium; 635.6mg potassium; 128.9g carbohydrates; 9.0g fiber; 48.0g sugar; 17.1g protein.

Gritty Nuts & Raisins

2	pkgs.	Instant Grits
1/3	cup	Raisins
1/3	cup	Pecans
1	cup	Water

Weight, 5.1 oz. | Cook, 5 minutes | Calories, 607

At Home

Using a permanent marker, write on a quart storage bag: the meal's name, amount of water needed, and cooking time. Now, place all of the dry ingredients in the bag.

Preparation

Measure the water into your pot and begin heating. Place the opened bag into your cooking hat. When the water boils, pinch one side of its "zipper" to hold it open while pouring the water in slowly. Press most of the air out of the bag and seal completely.

Tuck the bag into the hat and roll them together to prevent heat loss. Knead vigorously enough to mix the ingredients but not so hard as to pop the bag open.

Cooking

Let your meal cook in the hat for 5 minutes without peeking. Remix (i.e., knead) twice more during cooking time to ensure even distribution of water and ingredients.

When cooked, roll down the top of the hat to form an insulated bowl and enjoy.

Nutrition Facts

Nutrition: 607.0 calories; 37% calories from fat; 26.9g total fat; 0.0mg cholesterol; 615.9mg sodium; 642.7mg potassium; 92.7g carbohydrates; 8.2g fiber; 34.2g sugar; 9.7g protein.

Hang Dog

2	packs	Instant Cinnamon & Brown Sugar Oatmeal
1/2	cup	Banana Chips
1/2	cup	Semi-sweet Chocolate Chips
1 ¼	cups	Water

Weight, 9.1 oz. | Cook, 5 minutes | Calories, 946

At Home

Using a permanent marker, write on a quart storage bag: the meal's name, amount of water needed, and cooking time. Break the banana chips into smaller pieces; then place all ingredients in the bag.

Preparation

Measure the water into your pot and begin heating. Place the opened bag into your cooking hat. When the water boils, pinch one side of its "zipper" to hold it open while pouring the water in slowly. Press most of the air out of the bag and seal completely.

Tuck the bag into the hat and roll them together to prevent heat loss. Knead vigorously enough to mix the ingredients but not so hard as to pop the bag open.

Cooking

Let your meal cook in the hat for 5 minutes without peeking. Remix (i.e., knead) twice more during cooking time to ensure even distribution of water and ingredients.

When cooked, roll down the top of the hat to form an insulated bowl and enjoy.

Nutrition Facts

Nutrition: 946.6 calories; 38% calories from fat; 44.3g total fat; 0.0mg cholesterol; 538.1mg sodium; 788.7mg potassium; 142.4g carbohydrates; 10.3g fiber; 47.4g sugar; 11.9g protein.

Variations

This recipe is delicious if you are a full-fledged chocoholic. If not, save the chocolate chips to enjoy during a break – or eliminate them and subtract 321 calories from the day total.

This recipe is from *BACKPACKER*, April, 1996.

Instant Breakfast

1	pkg.	Carnation Instant Breakfast
4	tbsp.	Instant Nonfat Dehydrated Milk
1 1/4	cup	Water
1		Plastic Drinking Straw
2		Pop Tarts, Cinnamon & Brown Sugar (1 package)

Weight, 6.6 oz. | Cook, 0 minutes | Calories, 677

At Home

Using a permanent marker, write on a quart storage bag: the meal's name, amount of water needed, and cooking time. Repackage the Instant Breakfast, milk, and drinking straw in the quart bag. The Pop Tart package can either be packaged with the dry ingredients or Trail Boosters (i.e., snacks) depending on space restrictions.

Preparation

Place the zip bag in your hat for stability and add the water. Knead vigorously enough to mix the ingredients but not so hard as to pop the bag open.

When mixed, open one end of the bag's zipper, insert the straw, and enjoy along with your Pop Tart.

Nutrition Facts

Nutrition: 676.6 calories; 24% calories from fat; 18.6g total fat; 10.0mg cholesterol; 694.4mg sodium; 913.0mg potassium; 107.0g carbohydrates; 1.5g fiber; 59.0g sugar; 21.2g protein.

Note

You can make this a hot breakfast by heating (not boiling) the water before adding it to the Instant Breakfast (don't forget the hat!). You can also heat the Pop Tarts. Leaving them in their original packaging, lay them across the top of the pot as it heats, turning once or thrice.

Caution – Ideally, the Pop Tarts should not extend over the sides of the pot. If your pot is small and you are using an aluminum foil lid, unfold it enough to protect the wrapper from the direct heat flowing up the sides. If you don't, the wrapper will probably melt and/or burn no matter how vigilant you are. If combustion does occur, a spectacular expletive is the recommended signal for your shelter mates to give you their undivided attention and enjoy a good laugh.

Oatmeal Plus

2	pkg.	Instant Cinnamon & Brown Sugar Oatmeal
1/3	cup	Chopped Pecans
1/4	cup	Raisins
1 ¼	cups	Water

Weight, 5.8 oz.|Cook, 5 minutes|Calories, 689

At Home

Using a permanent marker, write on a quart storage bag: the meal's name, amount of water needed, and cooking time. Now, place all of the dry ingredients in the bag.

Preparation

Measure the water into your pot and begin heating. Place the opened bag into your cooking hat. When the water boils, pinch one side of its "zipper" to hold it open while pouring the water in slowly. Press most of the air out of the bag and seal completely.

Tuck the bag into the hat and roll them together to prevent heat loss. Knead vigorously enough to mix the ingredients but not so hard as to pop the bag open.

Cooking

Let your meal cook in the hat for 5 minutes without peeking. Remix (i.e., knead) twice more during cooking time to ensure even distribution of water and ingredients.

When cooked, roll down the top of the hat to form an insulated bowl and enjoy.

Nutrition Facts

Nutrition: 689.2 calories; 37% calories from fat; 30.5g total fat; 0.0mg cholesterol; 531.6mg sodium; 679.8mg potassium; 102.4g carbohydrates; 10.7g fiber; 52.0g sugar; 12.3g protein.

Note

I like instant oatmeal's flavor varieties, measuring is a no-brainer, and there is no difference in taste or texture between it and "quick oatmeal." Nevertheless, if quick is your preference, see the Quick Oatmeal Plus recipe below for additional ingredients and cooking time.

Quick Oatmeal Plus

1/2	cup	Quick Oatmeal
1/3	cup	Instant Nonfat Dehydrated Milk
1/3	cup	Chopped Pecans
1/3	cup	Raisins
2	tbsp.	Brown Sugar
1	tsp.	Cinnamon
1	pinch	Salt
1/2	cups	Water

Weight, 4.5 oz.|Cook, 7 minutes|Calories, 733

At Home

Using a permanent marker, write on a quart storage bag: the meal's name, amount of water needed, and cooking time. Now place all of the dry ingredients in the bag.

Preparation

Measure the water into your pot and begin heating. Place the opened bag into your cooking hat. When the water boils, pinch one side of its "zipper" to hold it open while pouring the water in slowly. Press most of the air out of the bag and seal completely.

Tuck the bag into the hat and roll them together to prevent heat loss. Knead vigorously enough to mix the ingredients but not so hard as to pop the bag open.

Cooking

Let your meal cook in the hat for 7 minutes without peeking. Remix (i.e., knead) twice more during cooking time to ensure even distribution of water and ingredients.

When cooked, roll down the top of the hat to form an insulated bowl and enjoy.

Nutrition Facts

Nutrition: 732.5 calories; 32% calories from fat; 28.0g total fat; 7.9mg cholesterol; 521.7mg sodium; 1366.6mg potassium; 108.9g carbohydrates; 7.5g fiber; 81.0g sugar; 21.8g protein.

Variation

For a chocoholic's breakfast or to turn this into an after supper treat, add 1/4 cup of semi-sweet or chocolate-peanut butter flavored morsels (280 calories) and omit the cinnamon. With chocolate added, they taste like the chocolate and oatmeal spoon cookies Mother made when I was a kid. Yum!

Rice Cherries

1/2	cup	Instant White Rice
1/2	cup	Instant Nonfat Dehydrated Milk
1/3	cup	Dried Cherries
2	tbsp.	Brown Sugar
1/4	tsp.	Cinnamon
1	pinch	Salt
5/8	cup	Water

Weight, 5.7 oz.|Cook, 10 minutes|Calories, 562

At Home

Using a permanent marker, write on a quart storage bag: the meal's name, amount of water needed, and cooking time. Now, measure the rice, milk, and salt into it. Place the cherries, brown sugar, and cinnamon in a sandwich bag and add it to the storage bag.

Preparation

Measure the water into your pot and begin heating. Place the opened bag into your cooking hat. Remove the sandwich bag of cherries, sugar, and cinnamon and place it in the hat next to the rice bag so it can warm while the rice cooks.

When the water boils, pinch one side of its "zipper" to hold it open while pouring the water in slowly. Press most of the air out of the bag and seal completely.

Tuck the bag into the hat and roll them together to prevent heat loss. Knead vigorously enough to mix the ingredients but not so hard as to pop the bag open.

Cooking

Let the rice cook in the hat for 10 minutes without peeking. Remix (i.e., knead) twice during cooking time to ensure even distribution and absorption of the water.

Before Eating

Open the bag and add the cherries, sugar, and cinnamon. Reseal and knead a few times to mix it thoroughly.

When cooked, roll down the top of the hat to form an insulated bowl and enjoy.

Nutrition Facts

Nutrition: 561.6 calories; 1% calories from fat; 1.3g total fat; 12.0mg cholesterol; 634.6mg sodium; 1177.8mg potassium; 115.5g carbohydrates; 3.4g fiber; 57.7g sugar; 24.7g protein.

Southern Cous

1/3	cup	Couscous
1/3	cup	Dried Peaches
1/3	cup	Pecans
1	pinch	Salt
1/2	cup	Water

Weight, 5.3 oz. | Cook, 5 minutes | Calories, 594

At Home

Using a permanent marker, write on a quart storage bag: the meal's name, amount of water needed, and cooking time. Now, place all of the dry ingredients in the bag.

Preparation

Put water on to boil and place zipper bag into your cook hat. When the water boils, open the bag and pinch one side of its "zipper" to hold it open while you pour the water in slowly. Press most of the air out of the bag and seal completely.

Roll the hat and bag together to prevent heat loss, and knead the ingredients thoroughly to mix. Knead vigorously enough to mix the ingredients but use care not to pop the bag open.

Cooking

Let your meal cook in the hat for 5 minutes without peeking. Remix (i.e., knead) twice more during cooking time to ensure even distribution of water and ingredients.

When cooked, roll down the top of the hat to form an insulated bowl and enjoy.

Nutrition Facts

Nutrition: 593.6 calories; 38% calories from fat; 26.9g total fat; 0.0mg cholesterol; 302.7mg sodium; 767.1mg potassium; 81.9g carbohydrates; 6.4g fiber; 1.4g sugar; 12.6g protein.

Tart Smoothie

1/2	pkg.	Instant Vanilla Pudding
4	tbsp.	Instant Nonfat Dehydrated Milk
1	tbsp.	Tang
1	cup	Water
1		Plastic Drinking Straw
2		Pop Tarts, Cinnamon & Brown Sugar

Weight, 6.5 oz.|Cook, 0 minutes|Calories, 779

At Home

Using a permanent marker, write on a quart storage bag: the meal's name and amount of water needed. Now repackage the pudding mix, milk, Tang, Pop Tarts, and drinking straw in the quart bag.

Preparation

Place the zipper bag into your cook hat for stability. Remove the Pop Tarts and set aside. Pinch one side of the bag's "zipper" to hold it open while you pour cold water in slowly. Press most of the air out of the bag and seal completely.

Roll the hat and bag together and knead the ingredients to mix thoroughly. Knead vigorously enough to mix the ingredients but use care not to pop the bag open. When mixed, open one end of the bag's zipper, insert the straw, and enjoy along with your Pop Tart.

Nutrition Facts

Nutrition: 778.9 calories; 21% calories from fat; 18.9g total fat; 6.0mg cholesterol; 1307.5mg sodium; 702.7mg potassium; 138.3g carbohydrates; 1.5g fiber; 98.2g sugar; 16.2g protein.

Note

Adjust the amount of water to obtain desired thickness, but remember that the pudding mix will continue to thicken the smoothie for about five minutes.

Saturday, June 15

I had a big week! My AT maps, tent, and pack cover were delivered. Every item that will accompany me on the trip is now in hand and I can schedule a shake-down hike This morning, the entire complement of gear was loaded for a neighborhood jaunt. I strapped on the pack and headed to the kitchen for the weigh-in. Sans food and water, it was heavy, unwieldy, and barely 26 pounds! The additional weight felt strangely compressing, particularly in my knees and hips.

Up until that moment, I had envisioned a great adventure with a few difficult moments, part-and-parcel for all true adventures. However, my overactive imagination encouraged the pack's compressing effect and strange unwieldiness to morph into 14 punishing days. My spiraling thoughts hit bottom as "Can I really do this?" reverberated behind my glazed-over eyes. The reality of having a fully-stocked house strapped to my back while walking up and down the Appalachian Mountains all day, every day, is dawning.

I've got to push harder in the gym and start training with a 40 pound pack.

Another pair of socks to test arrived in the mail Thursday, Thorlo's with heavy padding. The padding was too thick. Their medium weight socks are by far the best ones tried and will go on the trip. What am I going to do with the other $100 worth of socks I now have?

The next step is to test freeze-dried and dehydrated foods. I have been reading about and experimenting with breakfast ingredients for the last couple of weeks, but now I have to get serious about the whole eating thing (nutrition, ease of preparation, fuel economy, clean-up, variety, taste).

I have found little information beyond "use freeze-dried or dehydrated food because it is light" and "you need to get calories in a combination of 40% carbs, 30% fat, and 30% protein (or 60/20/20, or 70/20/10, or ...). Oh, by the way, how does somebody figure all that out?

I now understand why trail food authors consistently prescribe beef sticks, bagels, Snickers, and peanut butter. They are simple to pack and eat, and provide lots of calories. It seems that the magnitude of the caloric intake is more of an issue for most authors than the ratios of carb, fat, or protein calories. The general message is, "Focus on calories and hope you get close to an efficient and effective mix of energy sources."

Not finding a unified source containing weights, calories, nutrients, menus, etc. is surprising. Those are all issues that backpackers have been wrestling with forever.

Lunch

The best cure for insomnia is to get a lot of sleep.

W.C. Fields

On good days, lunch on the trail is a time to take a break; to remember walking the narrow trail cut into a mountain's chest where freckled sunshine was sending the morning's dew skyward. It is also a time to take your boots off, to wiggle your toes while you stretch out and simply enjoy *being*.

Other days, lunch is eaten inside an envelope of crashing rain. With no time for reflection, you hurriedly slosh toward a dry shelter while gulping down a soggy energy bar.

What you will find here are meals to meet your needs regardless of circumstances. Yet, backpackers are notorious for changing "a little here" or "a little there" to make meals their own (as we should!). To prevent adding unnecessary weight or omitting needed calories as you make modifications, use the *Table of Ingredients* in the back of this book as a guide.

Bacon, Cheese & Tomato Roll up

2		Flour Tortilla, 6 Inch
2	tbsp.	Real Bacon Bits
2	oz.	Cheddar Cheese Sticks
1/2	oz.	Sun Dried Tomatoes, Minced (five pieces equals 1/2 oz.)
2	packs	Mayonnaise

Weight, 5.78 oz.|Cook, 0 minutes|Calories, 679

At Home

Using a permanent marker, write the name of the meal on a quart bag. Measure the bacon bits and minced tomatoes into it. Then drop the individually wrapped cheese sticks and mayonnaise packets in. The tortillas should remain in their original packaging, or if only taking a few, packaged in a gallon zip bag.

At Meal Time

Spread mayonnaise on each tortilla, sprinkle on the bacon and tomatoes, and top each with a cheese stick. Roll up and enjoy.

Nutrition Facts

Nutrition: 679.6 calories; 62% calories from fat; 71.7g total fat; 69.5mg cholesterol; 1665.5mg sodium; 643.7mg potassium; 41.6g carbohydrates; 3.7g fiber; 6.9g sugar; 27.4g protein.

Bagel & Moose

1		Blueberry Bagel
2	tbsp.	Moose Goo (p. 122)
1/3	cup	Dried Apricots
1/3	cup	Walnuts

Weight, 9.8 oz.|Cook, 0 minutes|Calories, 785

At Home

Using a permanent marker, write the name of the meal on a quart bag. Measure the apricots and walnuts into it. Prepare a recipe of Moose Goo, and package it in a squeeze tube or plastic bag to be portioned when ready to use. Leave the bagel in its original package if you are going to take all of them. If not, repackage what you will take in a gallon bag.

At Meal Time

Squeeze the Moose Goo onto the bagel. The apricots and walnuts can either be imbedded in the Goo to make a HUGE sandwich or they can be eaten separately. I prefer some each way.

Nutrition Facts

Nutrition: 785.1 calories; 38% calories from fat; 71.4g total fat; 0.0mg cholesterol; 702.4mg sodium; 1268.2mg potassium; 214.2g carbohydrates; 20.5g fiber; 100.4g sugar; 40.0g protein.

Bean & Bacon Burrito

2		Flour Tortillas, 6 Inch
2	tbsp.	Real Bacon Bits
2	oz.	Cheddar Cheese Sticks
1/4	cup	Refried Beans (p. 132)

Weight, 6.8 oz.|Cook, 0 minutes|Calories, 547

At Home

Using a permanent marker, write the name of the meal on a quart bag and drop the cheese sticks and bacon bits in. The tortillas should remain in their original packaging or be placed in the gallon bag. The beans should be packaged in a squeeze tube to be portioned when ready to use or preportioned in a plastic bag.

At Meal Time

Spread half of the beans on each tortilla and sprinkle on the bacon bits. Top with cheese sticks, roll to make two burritos, and enjoy.

Nutrition Facts

Nutrition: 547.4 calories; 50% calories from fat; 54.5g total fat; 74.6mg cholesterol; 1447.5mg sodium; 323.0mg potassium; 43.4g carbohydrates; 5.3g fiber; 1.7g sugar; 28.9g protein.

Chick 'n Pot Pita

1	pkg.	Hearty Chicken Noodle Cup-a-Soup
2/3	cup	Instant Mashed Potatoes
1		Pita
1	tbsp.	Olive Oil
1	oz.	Cheddar Cheese Stick
1 1/2	cup	Water

Weight, 7.2 oz.|Cook, 5 minutes|Calories, 620

At Home

Using a permanent marker, write on a quart storage bag: the meal's name, amount of water needed, and cooking time. Now, measure the potatoes into the bag and sprinkle the soup mix in. Add the cheese stick in its original wrapper.

If taking all the pitas, leave them in their original package. If not, repackage what you will need in a gallon bag. The olive oil should be packaged in a squeeze bottle with a push-pull closure.

Preparation

Measure the water into your pot and begin heating. Place the opened bag into your cooking hat. Remove the cheese and set aside.

When the water boils, pinch one side of its "zipper" to hold it open while pouring the water in slowly. Press most of the air out of the bag and seal completely.

Tuck the bag into the hat and roll them together to prevent heat loss. Knead vigorously enough to mix the ingredients but not so hard as to pop the bag open.

Cooking

Let your meal cook in the hat for 5 minutes without peeking. Remix (i.e., knead) twice more during cooking time to ensure even distribution of water and ingredients.

When cooked, slice the cheese into the bag, reseal and knead to distribute it throughout. Wait one minute for the cheese to melt. Roll down the hat to form an insulated bowl, and enjoy with your pita.

Nutrition Facts

Nutrition: 620.0 calories; 35% calories from fat; 24.8g total fat; 44.0mg cholesterol; 1104.4mg sodium; 99.9mg potassium; 61.9g carbohydrates; 3.6g fiber; 1.1g sugar; 17.1g protein.

Cooking Tips

1 1/4 cups of water makes a thick meal, more like mashed potatoes. Use two cups of water to make it more like soup.

Mediterranean BCT

2		Pita
2	tbsp.	Real Bacon Bits
2	oz.	Cheddar Cheese Sticks
2	tbsp.	Sun Dried Tomatoes, Minced
3	packs	Mayonnaise

Weight, 8.7 oz.|Cook, 0 minutes|Calories, 692

At Home

Using a permanent marker, write the name of the meal on a quart bag and drop the cheese sticks and mayonnaise packets in. Place the bacon bits and tomatoes in a sandwich bag and drop into the quart bag. The tortillas should remain in their original packaging or if taking a few, pack in a gallon bag.

At Meal Time

Spread half of the mayonnaise on each pita. Divide the remaining ingredients between the pitas. Sprinkle the bacon bits and tomatoes on the mayonnaise so they will stick. Slice the cheese up into grater size pieces to top all. Fold the pitas over to form two sandwiches and enjoy.

Nutrition Facts

Nutrition: 692.4 calories; 40% calories from fat; 55.3g total fat; 73.3mg cholesterol; 1739.6mg sodium; 432.1mg potassium; 74.8g carbohydrates; 3.5g fiber; 5.3g sugar; 32.1g protein.

Mediterranean Calzone

1		Pita
2	oz.	Sliced Pepperoni Rounds
1	oz.	Mozzarella Cheese Stick
1	tbsp.	Parmesan Cheese
1	tsp.	Italian Herbs (e.g., Oregano, Basil)
1	tbsp.	Garlic Infused Olive Oil (p. 121)

Weight, 5.8 oz.|Cook, 0 minutes|Calories, 649

At Home

Using a permanent marker, write the name of the meal on a quart bag and repackage the pepperoni in it. Repackage the Parmesan cheese, herbs, and individually wrapped mozzarella stick in a sandwich bag and place all inside the quart bag. The pita should remain in its original packaging if taking all, or in a gallon bag if taking a few. The olive oil should be packed in a squeeze bottle with a push-pull closure and the beans, in a squeeze tube to be portioned when ready to use.

At Meal Time

Open the pita to form a pocket. Insert the pepperoni, slice the mozzarella and layer on top of the pepperoni, then sprinkle the Parmesan-herb mixture over the top. Finally, squirt your garlic infused olive oil over all, grab it with both hands, and enjoy.

Nutrition Facts

Nutrition: 648.7 calories; 60% calories from fat; 43.8g total fat; 88.6mg cholesterol; 1594.3mg sodium; 340.4mg potassium; 39.4g carbohydrates; 6.2g fiber; 1.4g sugar; 26.6g protein.

Mediterranean Moose

1		Pita
2	tbsp.	Moose Goo (p. 122)
2	oz.	Summer Sausage

Weight, 6.0 oz.|Cook, 0 minutes|Calories, 606

At Home

Prepare a recipe of Moose Goo and package it in squeeze tubes to be portioned when ready to use or preportioned in freezer bags. Leave the pitas in their original package if taking all of them. If not, repackage the needed amount in a gallon bag. Place the summer sausage in its own quart bag so it will have a home after the original wrapper is opened.

At Meal Time

Squeeze Moose Goo onto the pita and fold over. Either slice the summer sausage and add it to your sandwich, which is better than what you are probably imagining right now, or just eat it along with your "Gooburger."

Nutrition

Nutrition: 606.0 calories; 41% calories from fat; 82.4g total fat; 47.6mg cholesterol; 1747.3mg sodium; 1127.1mg potassium; 233.3g carbohydrates; 23.9g fiber; 95.6g sugar; 51.6g protein.

Mediterranean Pepperoni & Beans

1		Pita
2	oz.	Sliced Pepperoni Rounds (14 slices = 1 oz.)
1/2	cup	Refried Beans (p. 124)
2	tbsp.	Olive Oil

Weight, 9.0 oz.|Cook, 0 minutes|Calories, 658

At Home

Using a permanent marker, write the name of the meal on a quart bag then add the pepperoni. The pita can remain in its original packaging or if not taking all, packaged in a gallon bag. The olive oil should be packaged in a squeeze bottle with a push-pull closure, and beans should be packaged in a squeeze tube or plastic bag.

At Meal Time

Split the pita open; spread the beans on the bottom then add the pepperoni. Squirt the olive oil on the top so it soaks in. Flip the pita closed and enjoy.

Nutrition Facts

Nutrition: 657.8 calories; 56% calories from fat; 41.5g total fat; 43.1mg cholesterol; 1218.7mg sodium; 533.7mg potassium; 55.9g carbohydrates; 11.8g fiber; 1.0g sugar; 18.9g protein.

Mexican Fiesta

2		Flour Tortillas
1/2	cup	Refried Beans (p. 124)
2	oz.	Cheddar Cheese Sticks
1/2	oz.	Sun Dried Tomatoes, Minced (five pieces)
1/4	cup	Dried Apricots

Weight, 9.9 oz.|Cook, 0 minutes|Calories, 662

At Home

Using a permanent marker, write the name of the meal on a quart bag. Then repackage the cheese and minced tomatoes in a sandwich bag and drop it in the quart bag. Repackage the apricots in a second sandwich bag and add it to the quart bag. The tortillas should remain in their original packaging or be packaged in a gallon bag depending on the number taken. The refried beans should be packaged in a squeeze tube or plastic bag.

At Meal Time

Spread half of the beans on each tortilla, sprinkle on tomatoes and top with a cheese sticks. Roll them up to form two celebrations for your personal gratification.

The apricots can be eaten along with your tortillas or as dessert as you listen to the wind in the trees and contemplate how fortunate you are to be on the trail today instead of . . . well . . . *anywhere* else.

Nutrition Facts

Nutrition: 661.5 calories; 35% calories from fat; 25.9g total fat; 69.6mg cholesterol; 1436.1mg sodium; 1354.6mg potassium; 81.4g carbohydrates; 12.8g fiber; 24.5g sugar; 29.4g protein.

Mexican-Italian Roll Ups

2		Flour Tortillas
2	oz.	Sliced Pepperoni Rounds
1/4	cup	Dried Apples
1/4	cup	Salted Pistachios Kernels
2	packs	Mustard

Weight, 6.8 oz.|Cook, 0 minutes|Calories, 694

At Home

Using a permanent marker, write the name of the meal on a quart bag Repackage the pepperoni in it. Then repackage the apples, pistachios, and mustard packets in a sandwich bag, roll it up and place it inside the quart bag. The tortillas should remain in their original packaging or packed in a gallon bag so they remain flat.

At Meal Time

Spread a packet of mustard on half of each tortilla. Split the pepperoni between the two and roll them up to form two sandwich rolls. As you enjoy your roll ups, intersperse the apples and pistachios as sweet and salty contrasts to the bold blend of mustard and pepperoni. Chew slowly and try to picture what the breeze saw as it wound its way up from the valley floor collecting the wonderful fragrances funneled into your nostrils.

Nutrition Facts

Nutrition: 694.1 calories; 53% calories from fat; 42.0g total fat; 66.1mg cholesterol; 1663.6mg sodium; 707.9mg potassium; 58.3g carbohydrates; 8.2g fiber; 16.6g sugar; 23.9g protein.

Pocket Pizza

1		Pita
1	oz.	Sliced Pepperoni Rounds
1	tsp.	Italian Seasoning
2	tsp.	Parmesan Cheese
1	tbsp.	Olive Oil
1	oz.	Cheddar Cheese Stick

Weight, 4.9 oz.|Cook, 0 minutes|Calories, 546

At Home

Using a permanent marker, write the name of the meal on a quart bag; then add the pepperoni and cheddar cheese stick. Into a sandwich bag, measure out the Italian Seasoning and parmesan then drop it into the quart bag. The pita should remain in its original packaging or be packed in a gallon bag so it can remain flat. The olive oil should be packed in a squeeze bottle with a push-pull closure.

At Meal Time

Open the pita's pocket without completely separating the top and bottom. Stuff the pita with the pepperoni; then shave the cheddar cheese into it. Add the seasoning and cheese mixture, squirt the olive oil over all, grab it with both hands, and enjoy.

When finished with your sandwich, select four leaves, stems, fronds, petals, twigs, or other material from non-poisonous plants. Close your eyes and smell one – imprint the smell into your olfactory catalogue. Crush it, discover how the smell changes. Taste it – does it provide a spicy-minty burst like pansy stems or a pungent hickory taste? Describe it. A stronger, more personal connection to Nature is often acquired by continuing to experience Her plants this way. Perhaps you will too.

Nutrition Facts

Nutrition (per serving): 546.4 calories; 59% calories from fat; 35.9g total fat; 65.7mg cholesterol; 1050.1mg sodium; 192.3mg potassium; 35.7g carbohydrates; 1.9g fiber; 1.2g sugar; 33.8g net carbs; 19.6g protein.

Sausage Nuts Walking

2	oz.	Summer Sausage
2	oz.	Dried Apples
2	oz.	Walnuts

Weight, 6.0 oz.|Cook, 0 minutes|Calories, 681

At Home

Using a permanent marker, write on a quart bag the name of the meal and put the apples and walnuts in the bag together. Pack the sausage in its own *freezer* bag so it will have a home after being cut.

At Meal Time

Pull out your apple and nut bag, slice a 2 oz. piece off of the Summer Sausage stick and keep walking.

Nutrition Facts

Nutrition: 681.0 calories; 65% calories from fat; 52.3g total fat; 47.6mg cholesterol; 861.3mg sodium; 634.5mg potassium; 45.6g carbohydrates; 8.7g fiber; 34.2g sugar; 17.6g protein.

Notes

It is better to leave the sausage as originally packaged until needed. After opening, all of it should be eaten or discarded within three days during 3-season weather. If the temperature remains under 45°, it should be OK for several more days.

Sausage Tortilla Roll Ups

2		Flour Tortilla
3	oz.	Summer Sausage
2	oz.	Cheddar Cheese Sticks
3	packs	Mustard

Weight, 7.5 oz.|Cook, 0 minutes|Calories, 701

At Home

Using a permanent marker, write the name of the meal on a sandwich bag; then drop the cheese sticks and mustard packets in. The tortillas should remain in their original packaging if all will be taken. If not, package in a separate gallon bag. The entire summer sausage stick should be packaged separately in a *freezer* bag so it will have a home after it is cut.

At Meal Time

Spread the mustard on half of each tortilla. Slice the sausage, split it between the two tortillas, and top with a cheese stick. Roll the tortillas to form two sandwich rolls, and enjoy.

Nutrition Facts

Nutrition: 700.9 calories; 60% calories from fat; 47.2g total fat; 127.6mg cholesterol; 2138.3mg sodium; 375.6mg potassium; 36.4g carbohydrates; 2.5g fiber; 2.9g sugar; 32.4g protein.

Spam Sandwich

1		Pita
1	pkg.	Spam, 3 oz. single-serve foil pack
1	oz.	Cheddar Cheese
1	pack	Mayonnaise
1/4	cup	Raisins

Weight, 7.6 oz.|Cook, 0 minutes|Calories, 681

At Home

Using a permanent marker, write the name of the meal on a quart bag. Place the individually wrapped cheese sticks (or plastic wrapped chunk), packet of mayonnaise, and single-serve foil pack of Spam in it. The pita should remain in its original package if taking all, or packed in a separate gallon bag.

At Meal Time

Spread the mayonnaise on the pita. Open the Spam and squeeze it out from the bottom onto the pita. Cut the cheese into pieces and add it to the sandwich. Fold the pita in half and enjoy. Nibble on the raisins as dessert.

Nutrition Facts

Nutrition: 681.8 calories; 45% calories from fat; 34.8g total fat; 89.8mg cholesterol; 1686.5mg sodium; 601.5mg potassium; 70.1g carbohydrates; 2.8g fiber; 25.7g sugar; 25.0g protein.

Monday, June 17

My base weight jumped over my 25 pound limit when the tent was added. Without food and water, the pack weighs in at 26 pounds, 6 oz.

I had included the tent's "trail weight" of 3 pounds, 13 ounces (vs. pack weight of 4 pounds, 8 oz.; and fast pack weight of 2 pounds, 6 oz.). However, including poles, stakes, and rain fly (which are required to set it up and actually have it function as a shelter), it weighs a whopping 5 pounds, 2.7 oz.! I now have 15 lbs. 6 oz. in pack, tent, sleeping bag, and pad.

To move back to 25 pounds, the sleeping pad could be shortened so it ends just below my knees for 3 to 4 oz., swapping pots will drop 7 oz., one pair of extra socks instead of two saves 3 oz., eliminating a long sleeve shirt and wear fleece when I need sleeves drops 11 oz.

Together those cuts would total 24 oz. (1 lb., 8 oz.) and bring the total back down to 25 lbs. Serious consideration will have to be given to further reductions in comfort or flexibility.

Supper

Climb the mountains and get their good tidings. Nature's peace will flow into you as sunshine flows into trees. The winds will blow their own freshness into you, and the storms their energy, while cares will drop away from you like the leaves of Autumn.

John Muir

You have arrived at today's destination! Now is the time to relive what you experienced during the day, catch up on your journal, hear about your shelter mates' adventures as they straggle in, and enjoy a hot, tasty supper.

While breakfast and lunch are generally quick fuel for the body, supper is the meal we can take time to savor. It is a reward for accomplishing something that only a tiny portion of the population even consider.

Does Mexican, Chinese, Indian, or more standard fare suit you tonight? Fugedabout what is scheduled, select a meal that will make your mouth happy and enjoy. You've earned it!

Chicken Nuts & Rice

2/3	cup	Instant White Rice
1	pkg.	Chicken (3 oz. foil pack)
1/3	cup	Golden Raisins
1	tsp.	Onion Flakes
1/3	cup	Cashews, halves and pieces
1	pinch	Salt
2/3	cup	Water

Weight, 8.0 oz. | Cook, 10 minutes | Calories, 619

At Home

Using a permanent marker, write on a quart storage bag: the meal's name, amount of water needed, and cooking time. Now, measure the rice and salt into it. Package the cashews, raisins, and onion flakes in a sandwich bag. Place the sandwich bag containing the nuts and the foil package of chicken inside the quart bag.

Preparation

Measure the water into your pot and begin heating. Place the opened bag into your cooking hat. Remove the chicken and sandwich bag of nuts. Place the sandwich bag of dry ingredients and the foil pack of chicken in the hat next to the rice bag to warm while the rice cooks.

When the water boils, pinch one side of its "zipper" to hold it open while pouring the water in slowly. Press most of the air out of the bag and seal completely.

Tuck the bag into the hat and roll together to prevent heat loss. Knead vigorously enough to mix the ingredients but not so hard as to pop the bag open.

Cooking

Allow the rice cook in the hat for 10 minutes without peeking. Remix (i.e., knead) twice more during cooking time to ensure even distribution of water.

Before Eating

Open the bag and add the chicken, cashews and other dry ingredients. Reseal and knead a few times to mix it thoroughly.

When cooked, roll down the top of the hat to form an insulated bowl, and enjoy.

Nutrition Facts

Nutrition: 619.1 calories; 26% calories from fat; 18.7g total fat; 15.0mg cholesterol; 993.6mg sodium; 441.8mg potassium; 82.8g carbohydrates; 4.3g fiber; 35.9g sugar; 33.6g protein.

Chicken Tetrazini

1	pack	Chicken, Sweet Sue (3 oz. foil pack)
1	pack	Powdered Mushroom Gravy Mix
1	pack	Ramen Noodles (Discard flavor pack.)
1	cup	Water

Weight, 7.4 oz. | Cook, 8 minutes | Calories, 476

At Home

Using a permanent marker, write on a quart storage bag: the meal's name, amount of water needed, and cooking time. Now, place the mushroom gravy, noodles, and foil pack of chicken in it.

Preparation

Measure the water into your pot and begin heating. Place the opened bag into your cooking hat. When the water boils, pinch one side of its "zipper" to hold it open while pouring the water in slowly. Press most of the air out of the bag and seal completely. Place the foil pack of chicken in the hat next to the bag so the chicken can be warming while the noodles cook.

Tuck the bag into the hat and roll them together to prevent heat loss. Knead vigorously enough to mix the ingredients but not so hard as to pop the bag open.

Cooking

Let the noodles cook in the hat for 8 minutes without peeking. Remix (i.e., knead) twice more during cooking time to ensure even distribution of water.

Before Eating

Open the bag and add the chicken. Reseal and knead a few times to mix it thoroughly.

When cooked, roll down the top of the hat to form an insulated bowl, and enjoy.

Nutrition Facts

Nutrition: 476.3 calories; 33% calories from fat; 17.1g total fat; 15.0mg cholesterol; 1928.3mg sodium; 0.0mg potassium; 45.8g carbohydrates; 0.0g fiber; 0.0g sugar; 28.6g protein.

Crabby Alfredo

1/2	cup	Couscous
1/3	cup	Instant Nonfat Dehydrated Milk
1	pack	Imitation Crab (3.53 oz. foil pack)
2	tbsp.	Parmesan Cheese
1	tbsp.	Olive Oil
1	cup	Water

Weight, 8.5 oz.|Cook, 4 minutes|Calories, 671

At Home

Using a permanent marker, write on a quart storage bag: the meal's name, amount of water needed, and cooking time. Now, measure the couscous and milk into it.

Package the parmesan cheese in a sandwich bag, and drop it and the foil pack of clams into the quart bag. The olive oil should be packaged in a squeeze bottle with a push-pull closure.

Preparation

Measure the water into your pot and begin heating. Place the quart zipper bag into your cook hat. Remove the sandwich bag with the parmesan cheese and set aside. Situate the foil pack of crab in the hat so it can warm while the pasta cooks.

When the water boils, open the quart bag and pinch one side of its "zipper" to hold it open as you pour the water in slowly. Press most of the air out of the bag and seal completely.

Roll the hat and bag together to prevent heat loss and knead the ingredients to thoroughly mix. Knead vigorously enough to mix the ingredients but use care not to pop the bag open.

Cooking

Let the pasta cook in the hat for 4 minutes without peeking. Remix (i.e., knead) twice more during cooking time to ensure even distribution of water and ingredients.

Before Eating

Open the bag and add the crab, olive oil, and parmesan. Reseal and knead a few times to mix thoroughly.

When cooked, roll down the top of the hat to form an insulated bowl, and enjoy.

Nutrition Facts

Nutrition: 671.0 calories; 23% calories from fat; 17.7g total fat; 31.7mg cholesterol; 735.4mg sodium; 866.6mg potassium; 89.0g carbohydrates; 4.3g fiber; 20.7g sugar; 36.2g protein.

Curried Cashew Rice

1/3	cup	Instant White Rice
1/4	cup	Instant Nonfat Dehydrated Milk
1/3	cup	Cashews, Halves & Pieces
2	oz.	Cheddar Cheese
1	tsp.	Curry Powder
1	pinch	Salt
1/3	cup	Water

Weight, 5.5 oz.|Cook, 10 minutes|Calories, 637

At Home

Using a permanent marker, write on a quart storage bag: the meal's name, amount of water needed, and cooking time. Now, measure the rice, curry powder, salt, and milk into the quart bag. Package the cashews and cheese in a sandwich bag and add to the quart bag.

Preparation

Measure the water into your pot and begin heating. Place the opened bag into your cooking hat. Remove the sandwich bag of ingredients, set it and the cheese aside. When the water boils, pinch one side of the bag's "zipper" to hold it open while pouring the water in slowly. Press most of the air out of the bag and seal completely.

Tuck the bag into the hat and roll them together to prevent heat loss. Knead vigorously enough to mix the ingredients but not so hard as to pop the bag open.

Cooking

Let the rice cook in the hat for 10 minutes without peeking. Remix (i.e., knead) twice more during cooking time to ensure even distribution of water and ingredients. While the rice cooks, cut the cheese into pieces so it will be easier to melt and distribute throughout the meal. Add the cheese to the cashews as you slice it.

Before Eating

Open the bag and add the cashews and cheese. Reseal and knead a few times to mix it thoroughly.

When cooked, roll down the top of the hat to form an insulated bowl, and enjoy.

Nutrition Facts

Nutrition: 636.9 calories; 51% calories from fat; 36.7g total fat; 65.5mg cholesterol; 1007.1mg sodium; 626.9mg potassium; 42.5g carbohydrates; 2.3g fiber; 18.6g sugar; 35.7g protein.

Garlicky Shrimp Alfredo

1/2	cup	Couscous
2	tbsp.	Powdered Creamy Alfredo Sauce
1	pack	Shrimp, (3.53 oz. foil pack)
2	tbsp.	Parmesan Cheese
1	tbsp.	Olive Oil
1/2	cup	Water

Weight, 7.4 oz. | Cook, 4 minutes | Calories, 647

At Home

Using a permanent marker, write on a quart storage bag: the meal's name, amount of water needed, and cooking time. Now, repackage the couscous and alfredo sauce mix in the quart bag. Package the parmesan cheese in a sandwich bag, and drop it inside the quart bag along with the foil package of shrimp. The olive oil should be packaged in squeeze bottle with a push-pull closure.

Preparation

Measure the water into your pot and begin heating. Place the opened bag into your cooking hat. Take the shrimp out of the quart bag and place it in the hat next to the couscous bag so the shrimp can be warming while the couscous cooks. Remove the sandwich bag of parmesan cheese and set aside.

When the water boils, open the quart bag and pinch one side of its "zipper" to hold it open while you pour the water in slowly. Press most of the air out of the bag and seal completely.

Roll the hat and bag together to prevent heat loss. Knead vigorously enough to mix the ingredients but not so hard as to pop the bag open.

Cooking

Let the couscous cook in the hat for 4 minutes without peeking. Remix (i.e., knead) twice more during cooking time to ensure even distribution of water and ingredients.

Before Eating

Open the bag and add the shrimp, parmesan cheese, and oil. Reseal and knead a few times to mix thoroughly.

When cooked, roll down the top of the hat to form an insulated bowl, and enjoy.

Nutrition Facts

Nutrition: 646.7 calories; 31% calories from fat; 22.9g total fat; 182.4mg cholesterol; 717.3mg sodium; 346.5mg potassium; 72.5g carbohydrates; 4.6g fiber; 0.8g sugar; 34.8g protein.

General Athike

1	plank	Chinese Noodles
1	tbsp.	Hot & Spicy Szechwan Seasoning Mix
1	pack	Chicken, 3 oz. foil pack
4		Dried Shitake Mushrooms
1	pinch	Red Pepper Flakes
2	tbsp.	Olive Oil
2/3	cup	Water

Weight, 7.3 oz.|Cook, 8 minutes|Calories, 682

At Home

Using a permanent marker, write on a quart *freezer* bag: the meal's name, amount of water needed, and cooking time. Repackage the noodles, red pepper flakes, and Szechwan mix in the freezer bag. Cut each mushroom into eight to ten pieces and package them in a separate quart bag. Include them and the foil pack of chicken in the freezer bag. The olive oil should be packaged in squeeze bottle with a push-pull closure.

Preparation

At lunch, take the mushroom bag out and add 1/3 cup of water to rehydrate them before needed. They will rehydrate in two hours, but while you're in the food bag, it's a convenient time to get them out. Put the mushroom bag in an outside pocket of your pack or otherwise protect against the unlikely event that the bag will spring a leak.

When it's time to eat, measure the water into your pot and begin heating. Place the opened bag in your cooking hat. Place the foil pack of chicken and bag of *drained* mushrooms in the hat next to the noodles to warm while the noodles cook.

When the water boils, open the quart bag and pinch one side of its "zipper" to hold it open while you pour the water in slowly. Press most of the air out of the bag and seal completely.

Roll the hat and bag together to prevent heat loss. Knead vigorously enough to mix the ingredients but not so hard as to pop the bag open.

Cooking

Let the noodles cook in the hat for 8 minutes without peeking. Remix (i.e., knead) twice more during cooking time to ensure even distribution of water and ingredients.

Before Eating

Open the bag and add the chicken, mushrooms and oil. Reseal and knead a few times to mix thoroughly.

When cooked, roll down the top of the hat to form an insulated bowl, and enjoy.

Nutrition Facts

Nutrition: 681.5 calories; 39% calories from fat; 30.0g total fat; 15.0mg cholesterol; 1057.2mg sodium; 2.5mg potassium; 76.8g carbohydrates; 12.4g fiber; 0.0g sugar; 31.6g protein.

Notes

Use a freezer bag when packaging Chinese noodles to protect against their creating pin holes in the bag. These noodles have very sharp points when broken.

Leave the mushrooms out if you don't want to fool with rehydrating them, but, they do add a nice chewy, meaty ingredient to the meal. If you omit them, reduce the calorie count by 20 and weight by .2 oz.

Golden Brown Rice

1/2	cup	Instant Brown Rice
1/4	cup	Golden Raisins
1/4	cup	Peanuts
4	tbsp.	Fried Onions (1/4 cup)
1/2	cup	Water

Weight, 5.5 oz. | Cook, 15 minutes | Calories, 565

At Home

Using a permanent marker, write on a quart storage bag: the meal's name, amount of water needed, and cooking time. Now, measure the rice into the quart bag. Package the raisins and peanuts in a sandwich bag, and place the fried onions in a second sandwich bag to keep them from absorbing moisture from other ingredients and getting soggy. Place the sandwich bags inside the quart bag.

Preparation

Measure the water into your pot and begin heating. Place the opened bag into your cooking hat. Remove the sandwich bags and place next to the quart bag in the hat so the nuts and raisins will start warming while the rice cooks.

When the water boils, open the quart bag and pinch one side of its "zipper" to hold it open while you pour the water in slowly. Press most of the air out of the bag and seal completely.

Roll the hat and bag together to prevent heat loss. Knead vigorously enough to mix the ingredients but not so hard as to pop the bag open.

Cooking

Let the rice cook in the hat for 15 minutes without peeking (brown rice just takes longer to cook). Remix (i.e., knead) twice more during cooking time to ensure even distribution of water and ingredients.

Because it has to sit 15 minutes, keep it wrapped and out of any wind to prevent as much heat loss as possible. Unless the weather is cold and the wind is howling, it should be plenty hot when it is time to eat.

Before Eating

Open the bag and add the raisins and peanuts. Reseal and knead a few times to mix thoroughly.

When cooked, roll down the top of the hat to form an insulated bowl, sprinkle the fried onions on top, and enjoy.

Nutrition Facts

Nutrition: 595.1 calories; 37% calories from fat; 26.2g total fat; 0.0mg cholesterol; 244.8mg sodium; 540.3mg potassium; 80.0g carbohydrates; 5.6g fiber; 23.0g sugar; 15.0g protein.

Meat 'n Taters

2/3	cup	Potato Flakes
1	oz.	Jerky (Your favorite flavor)
1/2	cup	Instant Nonfat Dehydrated Milk
1	tbsp.	Onion Flakes
1/4	tsp.	Garlic Powder
1	pinch	Salt
1	pinch	Black Pepper (Eliminate if black pepper flavor jerky is used.)
2	tbsp.	Olive Oil
1 1/4	cups	Water

Weight, 5.6 oz.|Cook, 6 minutes|Calories, 661

At Home

Using a permanent marker, write on a quart storage bag: the meal’s name, amount of water needed, and cooking time. Snip the jerky into 1/4 inch pieces, more or less, with kitchen scissors (one ounce cut up equals 1/3 cup). Then put all of the dry ingredients into the bag. The olive oil should be packaged in a squeeze bottle with a " push-pull " closure.

Preparation

Measure the water into your pot and begin heating. Place the opened bag into your cooking hat. When the water boils, pinch one side of its "zipper" to hold it open while you pour the water in slowly. Press most of the air out of the bag and seal completely.

Roll the hat and bag together to prevent heat loss and knead the ingredients to thoroughly mix. Knead vigorously enough to mix the ingredients but take care not to pop the bag open.

Cooking

Let your meal cook in the hat for 6 minutes without peeking. Remix (i.e., knead) twice more during cooking time to ensure even distribution of water and ingredients.

Before Eating

Open the bag and add the olive oil. Reseal and knead a few times to mix it thoroughly.

When cooked, roll down the top of the hat to form an insulated bowl, and enjoy.

Nutrition Facts

Nutrition: 661.5 calories; 37% calories from fat; 28.1g total fat; 42.0mg cholesterol; 1434.4mg sodium; 1524.2mg potassium; 66.5g carbohydrates; 3.0g fiber; 37.3g sugar; 37.0g protein.

Mexican Rice

3/4	cup	Instant White Rice
1/4	cup	Refried Beans (p. 124)
3	oz.	Sweet Sue Chicken (3 oz. foil pack)
1	oz.	Cheddar cheese Stick, Individually Wrapped
3/4	cup	Water

Weight, 9.2 oz. | Cook, 10 minutes | Calories, 545

At Home

Using a permanent marker, write on a quart storage bag: the meal's name, amount of water needed, and cooking time. Measure the rice into the bag. Then add the individually wrapped cheese stick, and foil package of chicken. The beans should be mixed and packaged in a squeeze tube and portioned when ready to use or preportioned in a plastic bag.

Preparation

Measure the water into your pot and begin heating. Place the opened bag into your cooking hat. Remove the chicken and cheese stick and set aside. When the water boils pinch one side of its "zipper" to hold it open while you pour the water in slowly.

Place the unopened foil pouch of chicken in the hat next to the rice bag so it can begin getting hot while the rice cooks. Press most of the air out of the bag and seal completely.

Roll the hat and bag together to prevent heat loss. Knead vigorously enough to mix the ingredients but not so hard as to pop the bag open.

Cooking

Let your rice cook in the hat for 10 minutes without peeking. Remix twice more during cooking time to ensure even distribution of water and ingredients.

Before Eating

Open the bag and add the chicken, beans, and cheese. Reseal and knead a few times to mix it thoroughly.

When cooked, roll down the top of the hat to form an insulated bowl, and enjoy.

Nutrition Facts

Nutrition: 544.8 calories; 18% calories from fat; 11.4g total fat; 50.0mg cholesterol; 868.4mg sodium; 208.8mg potassium; 70.7g carbohydrates; 4.5g fiber; 0.3g sugar; 36.2g protein.

Potato Bacon Soup

3/4	cup	Potato Flakes
1/2	cup	Instant Nonfat Dehydrated Milk
2	tbsp.	Real Bacon Bits
1 1/2	tbsp.	Onion Flakes
1	tbsp.	Butter Buds
1	pinch	Black Pepper
1	pinch	Salt
1		Pita
1/3	cup	Water

Weight, 6.0oz. | Cook, 5 minutes | Calories, 650

At Home

Using a permanent marker, write on a quart storage bag: the meal's name, amount of water needed, and cooking time. Now, add all of the dry ingredients to the quart bag, except the pita. The pita should remain in its original bag if taking the entire package. If not, repackage it in a gallon bag with the other pitas you will take.

Preparation

Measure the water into your pot and begin heating. Place the opened bag into your cooking hat and dig a pita out of your food sack. When the water boils, pinch one side of its "zipper" to hold it open while you pour the water in slowly. Press most of the air out of the bag and seal completely.

Roll the hat and bag together to prevent heat loss. Knead vigorously enough to mix the ingredients but not so hard as to pop the bag open.

Cooking

Let the soup cook in the hat for 5 minutes without peeking. Remix (i.e., knead) twice more during cooking time to ensure even distribution of water and ingredients.

When cooked, roll down the top of the hat to form an insulated bowl, and enjoy with your pita.

Nutrition Facts

Nutrition: 650.0 calories; 10% calories from fat; 31.3g total fat; 22.1mg cholesterol; 1512.6mg sodium; 1180.2mg potassium; 91.4g carbohydrates; 4.0g fiber; 32.9g sugar; 35.7g protein.

Rice Jerky

3/4	cup	Instant White Rice
1	oz.	Teriyaki Flavored Jerky
1	pinch	Red Pepper Flakes
1	tbsp.	Olive Oil
7/8	cup	Water

Weight, 6.0 oz.|Cook, 10 minutes|Calories, 506

At Home

Using a permanent marker, write on a quart storage bag: the meal's name, amount of water needed, and cooking time. With scissors, cut the jerky into 1/4 inch pieces, more or less. (One ounce cut up equals 1/3 cup.) Now place all of the dry ingredients in the bag. The olive oil should be packaged in a squeeze bottle with a push-pull closure.

Preparation

Measure the water into your pot and begin heating. Place the opened bag into your cooking hat. When the water boils, pinch one side of the bag's "zipper" to hold it open while you pour the water in slowly. Press most of the air out of the bag and seal completely.

Roll the hat and bag together prevent heat loss. Knead vigorously enough to mix the ingredients but not so hard as to pop the bag open.

Cooking

Let your meal cook in the hat for 10 minutes without peeking. Remix (i.e., knead) twice more during cooking time to ensure even distribution of water and ingredients.

Before Eating

Open the bag and add the olive oil. Reseal and knead a few times to mix it thoroughly.

When cooked, roll down the top of the hat to form an insulated bowl, and enjoy.

Nutrition Facts

Nutrition: 506.0 calories; 36% calories from fat; 21.0g total fat; 13.6mg cholesterol; 636.2mg sodium; 184.5mg potassium; 62.7g carbohydrates; 1.7g fiber; 2.6g sugar; 14.9g protein.

Sausage Pot

2/3	cup	Potato Flakes
2	oz.	Summer Sausage
2	oz.	Cheddar Cheese
4	tbsp.	Instant Nonfat Dehydrated Milk
1	pinch	Red Pepper Flakes
1 1/4	cups	Water

Weight, 5.6 oz.|Cook, 6 minutes|Calories, 623

At Home

Using a permanent marker, write on a quart storage bag: the meal's name, amount of water needed, and cooking time. Now, add the potatoes, milk, red pepper flakes, and individually wrapped cheese sticks to the quart bag. The summer sausage stick should be packaged in a separate quart *freezer* bag so it will have a home after being cut.

Preparation

Measure the water into your pot and begin heating. Place the opened bag into your cooking hat. Take the cheese sticks out and set aside. Cut the sausage into 1/4 inch cubes and add to the dry ingredients.

When the water boils, pinch one side of the bag's "zipper" to hold it open while you pour the water in slowly. Press most of the air out of the bag and seal completely.

Roll the hat and bag together prevent heat loss. Knead vigorously enough to mix the ingredients but not so hard as to pop the bag open.

Cooking

Let your meal cook in the hat for 5 minutes without peeking. Remix (i.e., knead) twice more during cooking time to ensure even distribution of water and ingredients.

Before Eating

Slice the cheese into your meal. Reseal the bag and knead to mix in the cheese. Roll the top of the hat down to form an insulated bowl, and enjoy.

Nutrition Facts

Nutrition: 623.6 calories; 49% calories from fat; 34.3g total fat; 113.2mg cholesterol; 1363.7mg sodium; 1073.7mg potassium; 43.0g carbohydrates; 2.2g fiber; 17.3g sugar; 36.1g protein.

Three Cheese Tortellini

1	cup	Three Cheese Tortellini, Dried
2	tsp.	Powdered Spaghetti Sauce Mix
1 1/2	tbsp.	Sun Dried Tomatoes, Minced
1	tbsp.	Italian Seasoning
1	pinch	Red Pepper Flakes
1	tbsp.	Olive Oil
1	cup	Water

Weight, 4.5 oz.|Cook, 15 minutes|Calories, 537

At Home

Using a permanent marker, write on a quart storage bag: the meal's name, amount of water needed, and cooking time. Repackage all of the dry ingredients in the quart bag. The olive oil should be packaged in a squeeze bottle with a push-pull closure.

Preparation

Measure the water into your pot and begin heating. Place the opened bag into your cooking hat. When the water boils, pinch one side of its "zipper" to hold it open while you pour the water in slowly. Press most of the air out of the bag and seal completely.

Roll the hat and bag together to prevent heat loss. Knead vigorously enough to mix the ingredients but not so hard as to pop the bag open.

Cooking

Let your meal cook in the hat for 15 minutes without peeking. Remix (i.e., knead) twice more during cooking time to ensure even distribution of water and ingredients.

Before Eating

Open the bag and add the olive oil. Reseal and knead a few times to mix it thoroughly.

When cooked, roll down the top of the hat to form an insulated bowl, and enjoy.

Nutrition Facts

Nutrition: 536.5 calories; 42% calories from fat; 26.3g total fat; 60.0mg cholesterol; 2188.7mg sodium; 385.3mg potassium; 65.6g carbohydrates; 7.6g fiber; 3.6g sugar; 14.2g protein.

Note

Use Barilla's or other small tortellini. Larger tortellini (e.g., Wal-Mart's brand) is too big to fully cook in a reasonable amount of time.

Tofu Miso Noodles

1	plank	Chinese Noodles
1	pack	Tofu Miso Soup Mix
4		Dried Shitake Mushrooms
1/4	cup	Peanuts, Oil Roasted & Salted
2/3	cup	Water

Weight, 7.3 oz.|Cook, 8 minutes|Calories, 571

At Home

Using a permanent marker, write on a quart storage bag: the meal's name, amount of water needed, and cooking time. Dump the noodles, peanuts, and miso soup mix into the bag. Cut each mushroom into eight to 10 pieces, package them in a separate quart bag, and add them to the noodle bag.

Preparation

During lunch, take the mushroom bag out and add 1/3 cup of water to rehydrate them. Place it in an outside pocket on your pack so nothing valuable gets wet if the bag leaks.

When it's time to eat, measure the water into your pot and start heating. Place the opened noodle bag in your cook hat and add the drained mushrooms.

When the water boils, pinch one side of the bag's "zipper" to hold it open while you pour the water in slowly. Press most of the air out of the bag and seal completely.

Roll the hat and bag together to prevent heat loss. Knead vigorously enough to mix the ingredients but not so hard as to pop the bag open.

Cooking

Let the meal cook in the hat for 8 minutes without peeking. Remix (i.e., knead) twice more during cooking time to ensure even distribution of water and ingredients.

When cooked, roll down the top of the hat to form an insulated bowl, and enjoy.

Nutrition Facts

Nutrition: 570.6 calories; 32% calories from fat; 21.9g total fat; 0.0mg cholesterol; 971.6mg sodium; 261.4mg potassium; 79.7g carbohydrates; 15.8g fiber; 1.5g sugar; 24.7g protein.

Cooking Tips

Use a *freezer* bag when packaging Chinese noodles to protect against their creating pin holes in the bag. They have very sharp points when broken.

You can leave the mushrooms out if you don't want to fool with rehydrating them. But they do add a nice chewy, meaty ingredient to the meal. If you omit them, reduce the calorie count by 20 and weight by .2 oz.

<u>Tuesday, June 25</u>

Did my usual hour on the treadmill at the gym today. Almost all was on a 15% grade at 2.5 – 2.7 mph. However, the last ten minutes or so, I had to keep telling myself, "I can see the shelter . . . I'm almost there . . . I can do anything *for another 10 . . . 5 . . . 2 minutes."*

AT accounts often include reports of injuries to various joints (e.g., knees, hips, ankles) that force people off the trail. Today, for the first time, my hip joints felt unlubricated. The balls didn't glide in the sockets – instead they felt almost as if they were grinding. The increased grade that I walked today must be the culprit.

I can't back off because some mountains will be steeper and take more than an hour to crest. The norm needs to become a 15% grade – the stair stepper and weights will be integrated into the routine.

Next week the new regimen will be: treadmill on Monday, Tuesday, and Friday; weights on Wednesday; and the stair stepper on Thursday. The closer I come to being in trail-shape now, the more enjoyable (or less painful) the AT will be.

Dessert

You must do the thing you think you cannot do.
Eleanor Roosevelt

Cap off supper with dessert and maybe a hot cup of (fill-in-the-blank). You will find taste-treats here that require mixing, chilling, and adding toppings. Others, like the first listed (i.e., Brownie), need only to have its wrapper ripped off. However, unwrapping prior to inserting one into your oral cavity is strictly optional in the truest expression of becoming one with the wilds.

With or without wrappers, enjoy your deserts to the fullest. Don't just gobble them down (except for the Cheese Danish), but allow them to fill your mouth with decadent sensations as you savor your well earned respite and contemplate the morrow.

When packaging your suppers at home, add the accompanying dessert (and beverage mix/bag) to each meal's bag. That way, one bag has everything needed for a complete meal. Digging around in your food sack looking for different parts of a meal should become passé. Say it with me, "Easy is good."

Brownie

1	Brownie, Little Debbie

Weight, 2.0 oz.|Cook, 0 minutes|Calories, 228

At Home

Drop the brownie, in its original wrapper, into the quart bag containing the supper it will accompany.

Preparation

None (OK, you may want to unwrap it.)

Nutrition

Nutrition (per serving): 228.0 calories; 31% calories from fat; 8.0g total fat; 0.0mg cholesterol; 0.0mg sodium; 0.0mg potassium; 37.0g carbohydrates; 0.0g fiber; 0.0g sugar; 2.0g protein.

Cheese Danish

1	Kellogg's Cheese Danish, Individually Wrapped

Weight, 2.2 oz.|Cook, 0 minutes|Calories, 255

At Home

Drop the pastry, in its original wrapper, into the quart bag containing the supper it will accompany.

After Supper

Hurriedly stuff the danish in your face and wash it down with a steaming cup of coffee. You have something more important to do.

Finished? Grab a fleece top to roll up as a pillow and locate a nice spot of semi-level ground away from the shelter. Assume a prone position, will your muscles to relax, and with the eyes of a child watch the evening clouds form shapes and hues that will never be seen again.

For the next 15 minutes think about nothing except the sky and how your bed of moist earth smells. Let your imagination conjure up cottages, coastlines, continents, clowns, or corn dogs among the clouds. Into your core, breath the moist smells of earth, leaves, and wood melding into the thick layer of nurturing loam that is cushioning you.

Burn these images and smells into your consciousness. After you return to work, beam yourself back to that place and time whenever you need to.

Nutrition Facts

Nutrition (per serving): 255.0 calories; 38% calories from fat; 11.0g total fat; 0.0mg cholesterol; 0.0mg sodium; 0.0mg potassium; 36.0g carbohydrates; 0.0g fiber; 0.0g sugar; 3.0g protein.

Cherry Cheesecake

4	tbsp.	Instant Cheesecake Mix
1/3	cup	Instant Nonfat Dehydrated Milk
1/4	cup	Dried Cherries
2	tbsp.	Graham Cracker Crumbs (included with the cheese cake mix)
1	cup	Water

Weight, 4.47 oz.|Cook, 5 minutes|Calories, 731

At Home

Using a permanent marker, write on a quart storage bag: the dessert's name, amount of water needed, and chilling time. Add the cheese cake mix, dry milk, and cherries. Place the Graham Cracker crumbs in a separate sandwich bag and drop it into the quart bag.

Preparation

While you are waiting for supper to cook, prepare the cheesecake mix. Open the bag and pinch one side of its "zipper" to hold it open while you pour the water in slowly. Knead for two minutes, but be careful not to pop the zipper.

Chilling

Make sure the bag is sealed tightly, and prop it up in a nearby creek or spring to chill until you are ready for it. Take precautions to keep untreated water (with its wigglies and viruses) away from the zipper so it cannot enter the bag when opened. If you want to err on the safe side, put the bag in the shade, instead of a water source, and it will soft-set in five minutes.

Before Eating

Sprinkle the Graham Cracker crumbs across the top, smack your lips and enjoy one of the best deserts ever devised for back country living!

Nutrition Facts

Nutrition (per serving): 731.2 calories; 12% calories from fat; 10.4g total fat; 7.9mg cholesterol; 1101.0mg sodium; 738.7mg potassium; 136.6g carbohydrates; 2.5g fiber; 24.3g sugar; 25.4g protein.

Variation

Substitute 1 Tbsp. Granola or Grape Nuts for the Graham Cracker crumbs. If you do make a substitution, subtract 34 or 45 calories respectively.

Chocolate Mocha Pudding

1/2	pack	Instant Chocolate Pudding
2	tsp.	Instant Coffee
1/3	cup	Instant Nonfat Dehydrated Milk
1	cup	Water

Weight, 3.39 oz. | Cook, 5 minutes | Calories, 334

At Home

Using a permanent marker, write on a quart storage bag: the dessert's name, amount of water needed, and chilling time. Now, add all of the dry ingredients to the quart bag.

Preparation

While you are waiting for supper to cook, prepare the pudding. Open the bag and pinch one side of its "zipper" to hold it open while you pour the water in slowly. Knead for two minutes, but be careful not to pop the zipper.

Chilling

Make sure the bag is sealed tightly, and prop it up in a nearby creek or spring to chill until you are ready for it. Take precautions to keep untreated water (with its wigglies and viruses) away from the zipper so it cannot enter the bag when opened. If you want to err on the safe side, put the bag in the shade, instead of a water source, and it will soft-set in five minutes.

Nutrition Facts

Nutrition (per serving): 334.3 calories; 3% calories from fat; 1.3g total fat; 7.9mg cholesterol; 924.6mg sodium; 890.9mg potassium; 64.7g carbohydrates; 1.8g fiber; 54.2g sugar; 15.7g protein.

Chocolate Vanilla Pudding

1/2	pack	Instant Vanilla Pudding
1/3	cup	Instant Nonfat Dehydrated Milk
1/4	cup	Semi-sweet Chocolate Chips
1	cup	Water

Weight, 4.6 oz.|Cook, 5 minutes|Calories, 531

At Home

Using a permanent marker, write on a quart storage bag: the dessert's name, amount of water needed, and chilling time. Now, measure the pudding and milk into it. Measure the chocolate chips into a sandwich bag and add it to the dry ingredients.

Preparation

While you are waiting for supper to cook, get the pudding in the creek. Take the chocolate chips out and set aside. Pour the water into the quart bag, and knead for two minutes.

Chilling

Make sure the bag is sealed tightly, and prop it up in a nearby creek or spring to chill until you are ready for it. Take precautions not to get untreated water (i.e., wigglies, viruses) on top of the zipper where it will run into the mix when opened. If you want to err on the safe side, just put it in the shade and it will become soft-set in five minutes.

Before Eating

Dump the chocolate chips on top; mix'em if you want to and dig in!

Nutrition Facts

Nutrition (per serving): 531.1 calories; 19% calories from fat; 13.2g total fat; 7.9mg cholesterol; 934.5mg sodium; 716.4mg potassium; 93.2g carbohydrates; 2.5g fiber; 66.6g sugar; 16.1g protein.

Fig Newtons

3	Fig Newtons

Weight, 1.6 oz.|Cook, 0 minutes|Calories, 150

At Home

Repackage the Fig Newtons in a sandwich bag, roll up and drop into the quart bag that contains the accompanying supper.

Nutrition Facts

Nutrition (per serving): 150.0 calories; 0% calories from fat; 0.0g total fat; 0.0mg cholesterol; 375.0mg sodium; 0.0mg potassium; 66.0g carbohydrates; 3.0g fiber; 33.0g sugar; 3.0g protein.

Homesteader's Delight

1/4	cup	Dried Apples
1	tbsp.	Brown Sugar

Weight, 1.9 oz.|Cook, 0 minutes|Calories, 214

At Home

Using a permanent marker, write the name of the dessert on a quart bag. Repackage the apples and brown sugar in it. Seal the bag and shake it up to coat the apples. Open, squeeze the air out and reseal.

Preparation

Find a comfortable tree to rest your back against, relax and enjoy your well earned delight. Treasure the sweet juices filling your mouth after a day of drinking tepid water. Bask in the knowledge that today you easily accomplished feats that your boss cannot conceptualize.

Nutrition Facts

Nutrition (per serving): 213.6 calories; 0% calories from fat; 0.1g total fat; 0.0mg cholesterol; 24.1mg sodium; 144.3mg potassium; 27.5g carbohydrates; 1.9g fiber; 25.5g sugar; 0.2g protein.

Nutella Roll up

2	tbsp.	Nutella
1		Flour Tortilla

Weight, 2.1 oz.|Cook, 0 minutes|Calories, 288

At Home

Repackage the Nutella in a squeeze tube or plastic bag. The tortilla can be left in its original bag if all are going to be taken or repacked in a gallon bag with others you are taking.

Preparation

Spread the Nutella on the tortilla, roll to form a delicious nutty, chocolaty treat, and enjoy.

Nutrition Facts

Nutrition (per serving): 288.0 calories; 54% calories from fat; 18.6g total fat; 0.0mg cholesterol; 350.4mg sodium; 257.3mg potassium; 22.7g carbohydrates; 2.9g fiber; 3.6g sugar; 10.7g protein.

Oreo Pudding

1/2	pack	Instant Chocolate Pudding
1/3	cup	Instant Nonfat Dehydrated Milk
3		Oreos
1	cup	Water

Weight, 3.7 oz.|Cook, 5 minutes|Calories, 471

At Home

Using a permanent marker, write on a quart storage bag: the meal's name, amount of water needed, and chilling time. Then measure the pudding mix and dry milk into it. Place the Oreos in a sandwich bag and add them to the quart bag.

Preparation

While you are waiting for supper to cook, prepare the pudding. Take the Oreo bag out and set aside. Pour the water into the pudding mix bag; knead for two minutes.

Chilling

Make sure the bag is sealed tightly, and prop it up in a nearby creek or spring to chill until you are ready for it. Take precautions not to get untreated water (i.e., wigglies, viruses) on top of the zipper where it will run into the mix when opened. If you want to err on the safe side, just put it in the shade and it will become soft-set in five minutes.

Before Eating

Break up the Oreos (if they aren't already!) and sprinkle the pieces over the top of the pudding. Now, enjoy!

Nutrition Facts

Nutrition (per serving): 471.0 calories; 13% calories from fat; 7.0g total fat; 7.9mg cholesterol; 924.0mg sodium; 827.2mg potassium; 85.5g carbohydrates; 2.7g fiber; 66.4g sugar; 17.0g protein.

Rice Crispy Treat

1 Rice Crispy Treat, Little Debbie

Weight, 1.6 oz.|Cook, 0 minutes|Calories, 190

At Home

Drop the Rice Crispy Treat, as originally wrapped, into the quart bag containing its accompanying meal.

Preparation

Put the Rice Crispy Treat in your pocket, tuck your sitting pad under one arm, pick up your freshly brewed cup of coffee, and walk to the edge of the ridge. Find the perfect place, the one that maximizes the vista – move if you need to.

Sit. Shift around until comfortable; then allow your thoughts to come to a stand still. Close your eyes and focus on the cornucopia of smells tumbling around you as the cooling air tows them to their nightly gathering in the valley below.

Concentrate, isolate one scent, and identify its origin before moving to another: Is it wet rock? Dead leaves warmed by the sun? The smell of warm, damp fur - a deer, dog, bear!? An unhappy skunk over the ridge? Pitch oozing from the fir trees guarding your shelter? Isolate, concentrate.

With your eyes still closed … quietly unwrap your Rice Crispy Treat and take a small bite. Don't chew; let it begin to melt in your mouth …

Nutrition Facts

Nutrition (per serving): 190.0 calories; 13% calories from fat; 4.5g total fat; 0.0mg cholesterol; 220.0mg sodium; 0.0mg potassium; 35.0g carbohydrates; 1.0g fiber; 18.0g sugar; 29.0g protein.

Rocky Road

1/2	pack	Instant Chocolate Pudding
1/3	cup	Instant Nonfat Dehydrated Milk
1/4	cup	Tiny Marshmallows
1	tbsp.	Semi-Sweet Chocolate Chips
1	tbsp.	Chopped Walnuts
1	plank	Graham Cracker
1	cup	Water

Weight, 4.5 oz.|Cook, 5 minutes|Calories, 451

At Home

Using a permanent marker, write on a quart storage bag: the dessert's name, amount of water needed, and chilling time. Now, repackage the pudding mix and milk in the quart bag. In a sandwich bag, place the marshmallows, chocolate chips, and walnuts. Put the Graham Cracker in a second sandwich bag so it won't absorb moisture from other ingredients and become limp. Broken is OK; limp is not. Place all inside the quart bag.

Preparation

While you are waiting for supper to cook, get the pudding in the creek. Take the two sandwich bags out and set aside. Pour the water into the pudding mix bag, knead for two minutes.

Chilling

Make sure the bag is sealed tightly, and prop it up in a nearby creek or spring to chill until you are ready for it. Take precautions not to get untreated water (i.e., wigglies, viruses) on top of the zipper where it will run into the mix when opened. If you want to err on the safe side, just put it in the shade and it will become soft-set in five minutes.

Before Eating

Open the bag and stir in the chocolate chips, marshmallows, and nuts. Crumple the Graham Cracker on top, and enjoy a delicious treat!

Nutrition Facts

Nutrition (per serving): 450.9 calories; 21% calories from fat; 11.3g total fat; 7.9mg cholesterol; 614.5mg sodium; 834.3mg potassium; 72.3g carbohydrates; 2.4g fiber; 43.8g sugar; 18.3g protein.

Variation

Try substituting 1 tbsp. Granola or Grape Nuts for the Graham Cracker. If you make these substitutions, subtract 34 or 45 calories respectively.

Snickers

1 Snickers (2.07 oz. size)

Weight, 2.1 oz.|Cook, 0 minutes|Calories, 266

At Home

Drop the Snickers, as originally wrapped, into the quart bag containing its accompanying supper.

Preparation

None

Nutrition Facts

Nutrition (per serving): 266.2 calories; 36% calories from fat; 10.9g total fat; 8.0mg cholesterol; 130.0mg sodium; 184.1mg potassium; 36.8g carbohydrates; 1.4g fiber; 28.4g sugar; 5.2g protein.

Yogurt Covered Raisins

1/4 cup Yogurt Covered Raisins

Weight, 1.2 oz.|Cook, 0 minutes|Calories, 130

At Home

Repackage the yogurt covered raisins in a sandwich bag and drop it in the quart bag containing the supper it will accompany.

Preparation

Much of Nature's symphony was missed as you walked the trail today. Most hikers note the incomparable series of vistas, tiny fissures in elephant-size boulders nurturing a family of petite flowers, or the occasional bear. Few learn to hear the nuances that add rewarding shades of richness for those who listen.

Were you aware of the light breeze that rustled through the ferns to kiss your left cheek, the buzz of a hummingbird as it chased another from its nectar, the unceasing music the stream played for you as its waters hurried around rocks and limbs toward the Atlantic

Ocean, the squeak of two tree trunks as one strains to keep its aging parent from collapsing onto the forest floor, a squirrel's nut shavings bouncing on dried leaves, your boot brushing the grass along the edge of the trail, or the beat of your heart as you made your final, steep climb of the afternoon? Maybe tomorrow . . .

Grab your fleece, secure the yogurt covered raisins in the bottom of a deep pocket, and search out a comforting space away from the shelter to enjoy the evening. Have a seat. Stretch your legs out, and lean back against a tree.

Close your eyes and concentrate on nothing but what you hear. Begin separating distant sounds: cars, airplanes, wind in the valley but not up high where you are. After a few minutes, move your hearing to intermediate sounds: a squirrel being chased by his sister through the trees, the unintelligible mutter of conversation as your shelter mates swap stories and advice, the clank of a cook pot, or the brush of the protective crowns overhead. Now shift your focus to sounds that are close, like the spider preparing to swing from a twig into your ear ...

After making sure there really isn't a spider about to enter your ear canal, select the three plumpest raisins and pop them in your mouth. Begin to chew slowly, appreciating the blend of yogurt and raisin flavors and textures.

Did you hear the raisins screaming for help as you began chewing or were you too preoccupied with how they tasted? Focus, listen.

Nutrition Facts

Nutrition (per serving): 130.0 calories; 34% calories from fat; 5.0g total fat; 0.0mg cholesterol; 20.0mg sodium; 0.0mg potassium; 20.0g carbohydrates; 1.0g fiber; 19.0g sugar; 1.0g protein.

Rice Pudding

1/3	cup	Instant White Rice
1/4	cup	Instant Nonfat Dehydrated Milk
1/4	cup	Raisins
1	tsp.	Cinnamon
1	tbsp.	Brown Sugar
1	pinch	Salt
1/3	cup	Water

Weight, 3.9 oz.|Cook, 10 minutes|Calories, 344

At Home

Using a permanent marker, write on a quart storage bag: the dessert's name, amount of water needed, and cooking time. Then repackage the rice and salt in the quart bag. Place the rest of the dry ingredients in a sandwich bag, roll, and drop into in the quart bag.

Preparation

Measure the water into your pot and begin heating. Place the opened bag into your cooking hat. Take the sandwich bag of other ingredients out and set aside.

When the water boils, pinch one side of the bag's "zipper" to hold it open while you pour the water in slowly. Press most of the air out of the bag and seal completely.

Roll the hat and bag together to prevent heat loss. Knead vigorously enough to mix the ingredients but not so hard as to pop the bag open.

Cooking

Let the rice cook in the hat for 10 minutes without peeking. Remix (i.e., knead) twice more during cooking time to ensure even distribution of water and ingredients.

Before Eating

Add the other ingredients to the rice. Reseal the bag and knead to mix. Roll down the top of the hat to form an insulated bowl, and enjoy.

Nutrition Facts

Nutrition (per serving): 343.7 calories; 1% calories from fat; 0.6g total fat; 6.0mg cholesterol; 464.9mg sodium; 908.5mg potassium; 75.2g carbohydrates; 3.1g fiber; 53.3g sugar; 13.3g protein.

Tuesday, July 16

I went for a 3.1 mile stroll yesterday wearing a 35 pound pack for the first time. Walking was different but not taxing enough. From now on, the "training pack" will weigh 40 pounds – I need to stop talking about it and just do it.

The most hilly neighborhood circuit was followed, and surprisingly, it only took an hour. Even at half that pace (1.5 mph), walking to Fontana Dam (162 miles) in 14 days, including one zero day to resupply, is doable. It will require averaging 12.5 miles per day. Walking from 8 am till noon, take a half hour for lunch, then walking from 12:30 p.m. till 5 would do it (1.5 mph X 8.5 hrs/day = 12.75 miles). As a back-up, Wesser, NC is an alternative stopping point at 134 mi. (10.3 miles per day (mpd) with one zero day for resupply).

Anything you want is on the internet now, including sunrise and sunset times. For Georgia and North Carolina, sunrise and sunset will be about 6:50 and 8:00 p.m. EST (or 5:50 and 7:00 body time). Only 6 weeks to go!!

Trail Boosters

You can observe a lot just by watchin'.
Yogi Berra

What we eat between meals is just as important as the meals themselves. It is the totality of what we consume in a day that fuels us over the next ridge, or not.

I have seen people suck back a pack of Kool-Aid, or eat two or three pieces of hard candy before beginning a long ascent. Taking a "hit" of simple carbs (i.e., sugar) will certainly give you a quick burst of energy. Yet simple carbs eaten alone (and sometimes complex carbohydrates) can be counter-productive during a day of heavy exercise.

To be sure, the Trail Boosters listed here contain some sugar and complex carbohydrates. However, they are coupled with fats and proteins that break down slower in order to prevent your blood sugar, and therefore, your energy level, from spiking and crashing.

What follows are combinations of snacks that work in concert to help keep your feet moving all day. Unfortunately, since each day's Trail Boosters are just combinations of ready-to-eat "stuff," I couldn't think of catchy, descriptive names for each day's set. Therefore, I had to fall back on the convenient, yet mundane, "Trail Boosters #1," "Trail Boosters #2," etc. nomenclature. These names are not as descriptive as I would like for them to be, but until someone comes up with a better methodology, they will have to do.

At Home

Package all of your Trail Boosters in quart bags with the day it will be eaten on the outside (e.g., Day 1, Day 2); then pack all into a gallon bag(s). Five days' worth fits snugly into one gallon bag.

If you are not concerned with consuming an exact calorie count, package them ungrouped. With a little forethought, you can select a combination of Trail Boosters at breakfast that "sound good" and will provide the quantity and types of Booster calories needed during the day. Stuff them in pockets that are easily accessible while walking to encourage snacking between meals.

Trail Boosters #1

1	Harvest Bar, Toffee Chocolate Chip
2	Pop Tarts, Brown Sugar & Cinnamon (one package)
2	Slim Jims, (.97 oz. size)

Weight, 7.7 oz.|Cook, 0 minutes|Calories, 788

Nutrition Facts

Nutrition (per serving): 788.0 calories; 36% calories from fat; 51.4g total fat; 30.0mg cholesterol; 1388.0mg sodium; 135.0mg potassium; 113.4g carbohydrates; 6.5g fiber; 43.4g sugar; 24.4g protein.

Trail Boosters #2

1/2	cup	GORP, circa 1963 (p. 117)
1		Power Bar, Peanut Butter
1		Harvest Bar, Toffee and Chocolate Chip

Weight, 8.53 oz.|Cook, 0 minutes|Calories, 743

At Home

Mix GORP and portion a 1/2 cup servings into a quart sandwich bag.

Nutrition Facts

Nutrition (per serving): 742.9 calories; 23% calories from fat; 20.5g total fat; 0.0mg cholesterol; 380.7mg sodium; 436.7mg potassium; 123.3g carbohydrates; 9.1g fiber; 56.2g sugar; 23.2g protein.

Trail Boosters #3

2	oz.	Cheddar Cheese, 1 oz. individually wrapped sticks
1/4	cup	Sunflower Seeds
1/4	cup	Cashew Pieces
1		Cliff Bar, Chocolate Chip Peanut Crunch

Weight, 6.7 oz.|Cook, 0 minutes|Calories, 866

At Home

Mix the sunflower seeds and cashews together in a quart bag and drop the Cliff Bar and cheese sticks in.

Nutrition Facts

Nutrition (per serving): 865.9 calories; 56% calories from fat; 56.8g total fat; 59.5mg cholesterol; 917.5mg sodium; 440.1mg potassium; 60.6g carbohydrates; 9.9g fiber; 22.3g sugar; 37.9g protein.

Note

If you don't have individually wrapped cheese sticks on hand, slice 2 oz. off of a block of cheese and wrap it in plastic wrap, or put it in another quart *storage* bag before dropping it in. (If it is hot, the oil from the cheese will quickly seep through a sandwich bag.)

Trail Boosters #4

2	Pop Tarts, Frosted Chocolate Fudge (one package)
1	Harvest Bar
2	Slim Jims (.97 oz. size)

Weight, 7.0 oz.|Cook, 0 minutes|Calories, 255

Nutrition Facts

Nutrition (per serving): 752.5 calories; 27% calories from fat; 42.7g total fat; 30.0mg cholesterol; 1365.6mg sodium; 164.3mg potassium; 123.7g carbohydrates; 6.1g fiber; 57.5g sugar; 24.3g protein.

Trail Boosters #5

1/4	cup	Unsalted Sunflower Seeds
1/4	cup	Cashews Pieces
2		Harvest Bars

Weight, 6.8 oz.|Cook, 0 minutes|Calories, 887

At Home

Mix the cashews and sunflower seeds together in a quart bag and add the Harvest Bar in its original wrapper.

Nutrition Facts

Nutrition (per serving): 887.4 calories; 40% calories from fat; 42.0g total fat; 0.0mg cholesterol; 431.0mg sodium; 164.5mg potassium; 106.9g carbohydrates; 10.9g fiber; 38.0g sugar; 26.8g protein.

Trail Boosters #6

1	Snickers (2.07 oz. size)
1	Pria Bar, Mint Chocolate Cookie
2	Slim Jims (.97 oz. size)

Weight, 5.0 oz.|Cook, 0 minutes|Calories, 484

Nutrition Facts

Nutrition (per serving): 484.1 calories; 43% calories from fat; 42.7g total fat; 38.2mg cholesterol; 1043.8mg sodium; 189.6mg potassium; 56.9g carbohydrates; 4.5g fiber; 38.3g sugar; 22.3g protein.

Trail Boosters #7

1	Snickers (2.07 oz. size)
1	Power Bar, Peanut Butter
2	Slim Jims (.97 oz. size)

Weight, 6.3 oz.|Cook, 0 minutes|Calories, 606

Nutrition Facts

Nutrition (per serving): 606.2 calories; 34% calories from fat; 42.4g total fat; 38.0mg cholesterol; 1070.0mg sodium; 314.1mg potassium; 85.8g carbohydrates; 6.4g fiber; 44.4g sugar; 27.2g protein.

Trail Boosters #8

1	Power Bar, Peanut Butter
1	Cheddar Cheese, Individually Wrapped 1 oz. Stick
2	Pop Tarts, Cinnamon & Brown Sugar (one package)

Weight, 7.0 oz.|Cook, 0 minutes|Calories, 792

Nutrition Facts

Nutrition (per serving): 792.3 calories; 35% calories from fat; 31.3g total fat; 29.8mg cholesterol; 724.1mg sodium; 292.8mg potassium; 109.8g carbohydrates; 4.5g fiber; 41.5g sugar; 22.5g protein.

Trail Boosters #9

1	Cliff Bar
1	M&M Peanut, (1.74 oz. bag)
2	Slim Jims (.97 oz. size)

Weight, 6.0 oz.|Cook, 0 minutes|Calories, 593

Nutrition Facts

Nutrition (per serving): 592.5 calories; 40% calories from fat; 46.3g total fat; 34.2mg cholesterol; 1052.6mg sodium; 383.1mg potassium; 75.4g carbohydrates; 8.6g fiber; 43.9g sugar; 27.5g protein.

Trail Boosters #10

1	Cliff Bar
2	Cheddar cheese, Individually Wrapped 1 oz. Sticks
2	Slim Jims (.97 oz. size)

Weight, 6.3 oz.|Cook, 0 minutes|Calories, 579

Nutrition Facts

Nutrition (per serving): 578.5 calories; 51% calories from fat; 52.8g total fat; 89.5mg cholesterol; 1382.1mg sodium; 275.6mg potassium; 47.7g carbohydrates; 7.0g fiber; 20.3g sugar; 37.1g protein.

Trail Boosters #11

1		M&M Peanut (1.74 oz. bag)
1/2	cup	Tom Brokow's Granola (p. 118)
1		Cheddar Cheese, Individually Wrapped 1 oz. Stick

Weight, 4.9 oz.|Cook, 0 minutes|Calories, 657

Nutrition Facts

Nutrition (per serving): 657.1 calories; 52% calories from fat; 39.3g total fat; 34.2mg cholesterol; 232.6mg sodium; 197.8mg potassium; 61.0g carbohydrates; 5.2g fiber; 40.5g sugar; 17.7g protein.

Trail Boosters #12

1/2	cup	Seedy Granola (p. 120)
2		Cheddar Cheese, Individually Wrapped, 1 oz. Sticks
1		M&M Plain (1.74 oz. bag)

Weight, 6 oz.|Cook, 0 minutes|Calories, 1045

Nutrition Facts

Nutrition (per serving): 1044.7 calories; 53% calories from fat; 62.9g total fat; 66.3mg cholesterol; 447.4mg sodium; 183.2mg potassium; 96.9g carbohydrates; 8.2g fiber; 31.3g sugar; 28.2g protein.

Trail Boosters #13

3/4	cup	Mediterranean GORP (p. 118)
1		Snickers Marathon, Multi-Grain Crunch (1.94 oz. size)
1		Cheddar Cheese Individually Wrapped, 1 oz. Stick

Weight, 5.4 oz. | Cook, 0 minutes | Calories, 799

At Home

Make a bag full of Mediterranean GORP. Rough chop the apricots and crumble the bananas into smaller pieces. Place the fruit and nuts into a quart bag and mix.

Nutrition Facts

Nutrition (per serving): 798.8 calories; 48% calories from fat; 45.3g total fat; 34.8mg cholesterol; 555.5mg sodium; 1114.2mg potassium; 81.1g carbohydrates; 10.9g fiber; 49.3g sugar; 26.5g protein.

Trail Boosters #14

1/4	cup	Walnut Pieces
1/4	cup	Cashew Pieces
2		Pop Tarts Brown Sugar & Cinnamon (One package)

Weight, 5.8 oz. | Cook, 0 minutes | Calories, 809

At Home

Measure the walnuts and cashews into a quart bag and add the Pop Tarts in their original packaging .

Nutrition Facts

Nutrition (per serving): 809.3 calories; 53% calories from fat; 50.5g total fat; 0.0mg cholesterol; 578.6mg sodium; 264.0mg potassium; 78.4g carbohydrates; 4.5g fiber; 28.2g sugar; 16.9g protein.

Wednesday, July 17

The trip has to be postponed one week. My siblings and I scheduled Mother and Daddy's 60th anniversary party for Sunday, September 1, the day I was to leave Springer. I need to leave on a weekend so Martha can pick me up on a weekend – maybe I can wait one more week without my head exploding …

At an even 200 pounds, the scales registered a seven-year low yesterday. My goal is to reach 195 pounds before leaving so I do not have to haul five extra pounds up and down mountains for two weeks.

I walked 3.1 miles in an hour carrying 35 pounds Monday and Tuesday. Today, the pack weighed 40 pounds and the same circuit took 55 minutes.

Monday, no problem. Tuesday, I had hot-spots on the balls of both feet and the bottoms of my big toes. Wednesday, more of the same problems. Today I am going to wear the same socks as yesterday, carry the same weight, and test the addition of polypropylene sock liners.

Ingredient and Bonus Recipes

What is the use of a house if you haven't got a tolerable planet to put it on?

Henry David Thoreau

This is *Travel Light's* overflow chapter. It contains recipes for ingredients used in preceding recipes and additional recipes you might also enjoy. My hope is that you find a favorite among them that will power you over a lifetime of mountains.

Daniel Bars

2	cups	Rolled Oats
1/2	cup	Butter
1/2	cup	Brown Sugar
1/4	cup	Honey
1/2	cup	Raisins
1/2	cup	Craisins
1/2	cup	Walnuts

Weight, 23.2 oz.|Cook, 0 minutes|Calories, 2,431

At Home

Measure the oats, fruit, and nuts into a bowl and set aside. Add the butter to a sauce pan, and melt over medium-low heat. Stir in the brown sugar and honey until the brown sugar has dissolved. Pour over dry ingredients and mix thoroughly. Bake at 350° for about 30 minutes or until the mixture begins to brown.

When cooled, cut into 8 bars weighing 2.9 oz. (precooked wt.), which will provide 304 calories each.

Nutrition Facts

Nutrition (total recipe): 2,431.0 calories; 48% calories from fat; 135.0g total fat; 244.0mg cholesterol; 583.3mg sodium; 1465.6mg potassium; 315.9g carbohydrates; 11.1g fiber; 243.1g sugar; 304.8g net carbs; 18.3g protein

Recipe from *BACKPACKER*, May, 2000.

GORP, Circa 1963

2	cups	Cheerios
1	cup	Raisins
1	cup	M&M Plain
1	cup	Spanish Peanuts

Weight, 19.4 oz.|Cook, 0 minutes|Calories, 2,597

At Home

Combine all ingredients in a gallon bag to mix. Then separate serving into quart bags. The yield is approximately 5 cups, which equates to 20, 1/4 cup portions weighing .97 oz., providing 130 calories each.

Nutrition Facts

Nutrition (total recipe): 2,597.0 calories; 39% calories from fat; 118.3g total fat; 29.1mg cholesterol; 573.3mg sodium; 3014.4mg potassium; 355.9g carbohydrates; 26.0g fiber; 124.1g sugar; 329.8g net carbs; 58.2g protein.

Note

I learned this recipe as a Tenderfoot Scout in 1963. We called it Bird Seed, that led to some pitiful looks when given to hungry boys. More than one asked if they could eat it instead of feeding it to the birds!

GORP, Mediterranean

1/4	cup	Dried Apricots
1/4	cup	Banana Chips
1/3	cup	Dry Roasted Pistachios Kernels w/salt

Weight, 3.9 oz.|Cook, 0 minutes|Calories, 465

At Home

Rough chop the apricots and crumble the banana chips into smaller pieces. Place the fruit and nuts into a quart bag and mix. The yield is approximately 3/4 cup.

Nutrition Facts

Nutrition (total recipe): 464.6 calories; 52% calories from fat; 28.9g total fat; 0.0mg cholesterol; 169.4mg sodium; 961.4mg potassium; 48.7g carbohydrates; 8.9g fiber; 31.1g sugar; 39.9g net carbs; 10.5g protein.

Tom Brokaw's Granola

1	cup	Pitted Dates
4	cups	Rolled Oatmeal
1	cup	Shredded Coconut
1	cup	Pine Nuts
1	cup	Wheat Germ
1/3	cup	Sesame Seeds
1/2	cup	Honey
1/2	cup	Vegetable Oil

Weight, 41.4 oz.|Cook, 25 minutes|Calories, 3,874

At Home

Snip dates into small pieces and set aside. Combine other dry ingredients in a large bowl. In a sauce pan, stir together honey and oil and heat to a boil. Pour over dry ingredients and mix.

Spread onto two 10"x15" sheet pans. Bake 25 minutes at 325°, stirring occasionally. Add the fruit when cooled sufficiently.

The yield is approximately 8 1/3 cups, which equates to 24, 1/4 cup portions weighing 1.3 oz., providing 116 calories each.

Note

The recipe includes the following variations: substitute walnuts for pine nuts; substitute prunes, raisins or other fruit for the dates.

Nutrition Facts

Nutrition (total recipe): 3874.1 calories; 45% calories from fat; 205.0g total fat; 0.0mg cholesterol; 293.5mg sodium; 2997.7mg potassium; 497.9g carbohydrates; 58.6g fiber; 292.2g sugar; 439.2g net carbs; 66.0g protein

Recipe from www.gorp.away.com

Hazelnut Granola

4	cups	Oatmeal
1	cup	Hazelnuts, Roasted & Chopped
1	cup	Flaked Coconut
1/2	cup	Wheat Germ
1	cup	Raisins
2/3	cup	Honey
1	Tbsp.	Water
1	Tsp.	Vanilla
2	Tbsp.	Vegetable Oil

Weight, 35.6 oz.|Cook, 25 minutes|Calories, 3,395

At Home

Put oatmeal, hazelnuts, coconut, and wheat germ in a bowl, and mix lightly. Stir together honey, water, vanilla, and oil. Combine well with dry mixture. Spread in a 3-quart, lightly oiled baking pan.

Bake at 325° for 20-25 minutes, stirring every 5 minutes. Add raisins after sufficiently cooled.

Separate into quart storage bags. One-half cup weighs 2.4 oz., providing 226.3 calories.

Nutrition Facts

Nutrition (total recipe): 3395.1 calories; 37% calories from fat; 147.2g total fat; 0.0mg cholesterol; 278.4mg sodium; 2967.9mg potassium; 514.7g carbohydrates; 45.5g fiber; 328.9g sugar; 469.2g net carbs; 58.9g protein.

Recipe from: www.foodreference.com

Seedy Granola

5	cups	Rolled Oats
1/2	cup	Wheat Germ
1/4	cup	Sunflower Seeds
1/4	cup	Sesame Seeds
1/4	cup	Walnuts
2	tsp.	Cinnamon
1/2	cup	Honey
1/2	cup	Apple Juice
2	tbsp.	Canola Oil
1/2	cup	Dried Apricots, Chopped
1/2	cup	Dried Apples, Chopped

Weight, 36.8 oz. | Cook, 25 minutes | Calories, 2,694

At Home

Mix oats, wheat germ, seeds, nuts, and cinnamon in a large bowl. In a smaller bowl, combine the honey, apple juice, and oil. Pour liquid over dry ingredients and mix making sure to thoroughly coat dry ingredients.

Spread onto a baking sheet coated with nonstick cooking spray. Place in a preheated, 325° oven and bake for 20-25 minutes, or until browned, stirring three or four times.

Nutrition Information

Nutrition (per recipe): 2,694.2 calories; 32% calories from fat; 101.3g total fat; 0.0mg cholesterol; 1556.4mg sodium; 2526.4mg potassium; 439.8g carbohydrates; 38.9g fiber; 242.5g sugar; 400.9g net carbs; 47.5g protein.

Recipe from http://www.recipegoldmine.com

Note For an interesting history about granola's heritage, beginning in the early 1800s, go to: http://www.foodreference.com/html/artgranola.html

Garlic Infused Olive Oil

1/2	cup	Olive Oil
1	clove	Fresh Garlic, Sliced

Weight, 3.84 oz.|Cook, 2 minutes|Calories, 2,000

At Home

Infuse your olive oil with garlic for a delicious layer of flavor. Heat ½ cup of olive oil in a small sauté or sauce pan. While the oil is heating, peel and slice one clove of garlic.

When the oil begins to get fragrant (i.e., you start smelling it), add the garlic and cook for two minutes. (Burned garlic is bitter, so don't leave it.) Remove from heat.

When cooled sufficiently, remove the garlic and pour the oil into a squeeze bottle. If you want a more pronounced garlic flavor, add a second clove.

If you are feeling lucky, try pouring it directly from the pan into your squeeze bottle. If not, pour it back into the measuring cup first, then from the measuring cup into the squeeze bottle.

Note

You can also infuse olive oil with any fresh herb. Basil, rosemary, oregano, and thyme are some that are often enjoyed. Remember to strain the oil before pouring it into your squeeze bottle so the herbs do not clog the spout.

Nutrition Facts

Nutrition (total recipe): 2,000 calories; 100% calories from fat; 108.0g total fat; 0.0mg cholesterol; 3.2mg sodium; 1.1mg potassium; 0.0g carbohydrates; 0.0g fiber; 0.0g sugar; 0.0g net carbs; 0.0g protein.

Original Moose Goo

1	cup	Honey
1	cup	Corn Flour (not corn meal)
1/2	cup	Smooth Peanut Butter

Weight, 18.3 oz.|Cook, 0 minutes|Calories, 2,211

At Home

Place honey and peanut butter into a mixing bowl and mix thoroughly. Add corn flour and mix until smooth.

The yield is approximately 2 1/2 cups, which equates to approximately 5 squeeze tubes weighing 3.7 oz., providing 462 calories each.

Nutrition Facts

Nutrition (total recipe): 2,211.4 calories; 26% calories from fat; 69.5g total fat; 0.0mg cholesterol; 611.5mg sodium; 1382.0mg potassium; 394.5g carbohydrates; 19.6g fiber; 291.0g sugar; 374.8g net carbs; 41.5g protein.

Recipe is Ultralight Joe's, www.ultralightbackpacker.com

Moose Goo Two

1	cup	Smooth Peanut Butter
1	cup	Honey
1/2	cup	Shredded Coconut
1/4	cup	Peanut Oil

Weight, 24.6 oz.|Cook, 0 minutes|Calories, 3,258

At Home

Place peanut oil and peanut butter into a mixing bowl and mix thoroughly. Add honey and coconut, mix until smooth.

The yield is approximately 2 1/2 cups, which equates to approximately 5 squeeze tubes weighing 4.9 oz., providing 652 calories.

Nutrition Facts

Nutrition (total recipe): 3,257.9 calories; 52% calories from fat; 200.5g total fat; 0.0mg cholesterol; 1319.6mg sodium; 2007.4mg potassium; 352.0g carbohydrates; 18.3g fiber; 322.2g sugar; 333.7g net carbs; 67.1g protein.

NOLS Granola

5	tbsp.	Margarine
3	cups	Oatmeal
1/2	cup	Brown Sugar
1/2	tsp.	Salt
1/2	cup	Dried Apples
1/2	cup	Raisins
1/2	cup	Walnuts
1/2	cup	Sesame Seeds

Weight, 21.1 oz.|Cook, 15 minutes|Calories, 2,491

At Home

In a four-quart boiler, melt margarine on medium heat. When margarine is hot, add all other ingredients and stir to coat. Continue cooking until the oatmeal is golden brown, stirring frequently.

Alternatively, after all ingredients are coated with the margarine, dump contents out of the boiler onto a cookie sheet. Spread evenly and place in a preheated 350° oven. Bake for 20-25 minutes or until the oatmeal is golden brown. Stir frequently during the baking process.

The yield is approximately 5 1/2 cups, which equates to 22, 1/4 cup portions weighing .95 oz., providing 113 calories.

Nutrition Facts

Nutrition (total recipe): 2490.8 calories; 47% calories from fat; 139.2g total fat; 62.5mg cholesterol; 1898.1mg sodium; 1812.8mg potassium; 304.1g carbohydrates; 31.2g fiber; 181.0g sugar; 272.9g net carbs; 40.2g protein.

Recipe from *NOLS Cookery* (2004), 5th Edition

Power Peanut Butter

1/2	cup	Smooth Peanut Butter
1/4	cup	Honey
1/4	cup	Margarine
1/3	cup	Instant Nonfat Dehydrated Milk

Weight, 10.3 oz.|Cook, 0 minutes|Calories, 1,568

At Home

In a small boiler, heat peanut butter over medium-low heat. When it has melted, add remaining ingredients and combine. Let cool and pack into a squeeze tube or similar container.

The yield is approximately 1 cup, which equates to 4, 1/4 cup portions weighing 2.6 oz., providing 392 calories.

Nutrition Facts

Nutrition (total recipe): 1568.4 calories; 60% calories from fat; 111.1g total fat; 57.9mg cholesterol; 1318.5mg sodium; 1619.3mg potassium; 116.2g carbohydrates; 7.9g fiber; 102.3g sugar; 108.3g net carbs; 47.6g protein.

Recipe from *NOLS Cookery* (2004), 5th Edition

Refried Beans

1	cup	Canned Refried Beans
2	tbsp	Chili Powder
1	tsp.	Red Pepper Flakes
2	tsp.	Onion Flakes
1	tsp.	Cumin Seeds

Weight, 9.2 oz.|Cook, 0 minutes|Calories, 115

At Home

Place beans and 1/2 of each spice into a medium size bowl. Mix thoroughly, taste, and wait a minute for your mouth to get a good sense of what you just put in it. Now, based on your mouth's feedback, add some or all of the remaining ingredients. (You can also throw a little cilantro in if it will make your mouth happy.)

Pack the seasoned beans into a squeeze tube. You should be able to get a scant cup into a tube and still have room to seal it. The beans can also be packed as individual servings in pint storage bags if you do not happen to have any tubes handy. To use, either cut off a bottom corner and squeeze the beans out like a chef using a pastry bag, or spoon them out.

Nutrition Facts

Nutrition (per tube*): 114.8 calories; 13% calories from fat; 1.9g total fat; 9.1mg cholesterol; 438.0mg sodium; 352.6mg potassium; 19.0g carbohydrates; 6.9g fiber; 0.4g sugar; 12.1g net carbs; 6.5g protein.

* Servings per tube will vary according to how much individual recipes call for.

<u>Tuesday, August 20</u>

I discovered ultralight equipment a few weeks ago. There are packs weighing less than 2 pounds that will carry up to 30 lbs.! One tent has a third more floor space than the one I bought and is 3 lbs. lighter! The pack is more than 4 lbs. lighter than mine. These two items alone would reduce my base-weight 28%. A whole new world is revealing itself.

A ton of money was spent on gear before being sufficiently informed. Only recently did my thinking transition from car/boat/canoe camping, where weight means little, to a backpacking mentality, where weight is paramount.

The more acclimated I become to thinking "weight," the more meaningful 2 or 3 oz. becomes. An oz. added to pack weight is becoming like 5 seconds in the computer world. Depending on perspective, small things can become huge.

After replacing a few things with "ultra-light" versions, my pack weight is down to 19 lbs, 7 oz.!!!! What is amazing is there are still <u>pounds</u> to cut … a lighter sleeping bag … a lighter stove …

Martha gave me a pair of 8.7 oz. hiking pants for my birthday (today). They replace the 16.3 oz.

convertible pants I was going to take and will save almost a half-pound! That reduction makes room for a pair of 7.2 oz. rain pants, which can also be worn over shorts or the hiking pants for warmth. In total I still save .4 oz. – excellent!

I am finished with trimming weight with the exception of shortening the legs of my shorts and pants (how much weight will that save?). Mmmmm, I wonder, how much less food (i.e., calories) I can take since the total weight is considerably less than originally calculated …

Aaaaaaaahhhh! Stop me!! I'm obsessed*!!!*

Table of Equivalents

If you look at life at 50 the same way you did at 20, you've wasted 30 years.

Mohammed Ali

1 Tablespoon (tbsp.) = 3 Teaspoons (tsp.)

1 Fluid Ounce (fl. oz.) = 2 tbsp. = 6 tsp.

1/2 Cup (c) = 8 tbsp.

1 c = 8 oz. = 16 tbsp. = 236 ml

1 Pint (pt.)= 2 c. = 16 fl. oz. = 473 ml

1 Quart (qt.) = 4 c. = 2 pt. = 32 fl. oz. = 946 ml

1 Gallon (gal.) = 16 c. = 8 pt. = 4 qts. = 128 fl. oz. = 3.78 Liter (L)

1 Pound (lb.)= 16 oz. = 454 g

For those who don't have a measuring cup handy, here are some ways to approximate volume.

Item	**Approximation**
1 cup	• Tennis ball • Fist of an average adult
1/2 cup	• A cupcake wrapper • Half of a baseball
1/3 cup of nuts	• A level handful
1/4 cup	• A golf ball • A scant handful
2 tbsp. of peanut butter	• Ping-pong ball
1 ounce of cheese	• Two dominos • Four dice

American Institute of Cancer Research (2001)

<u>Monday, August 26</u>

I lied. I am still working on reducing pack weight while maintaining comfort and safety. I have been below 18 pounds, then back up, then back down ... This morning my pack weighs 18 pounds, 3 oz. I will continue to tweak things until I strap it on September 7 and have Springer Mountain at my back. It is amazing how little you actually need once you get into a light weight mind-set.

Less than two weeks to go!!!!

Note

I never envision being a minimalist. There is a threshold of physical and psychological comfort that I am simply not willing to cross. Even so, weight reductions continue, although not as aggressively as early on.

Currently, my 3-season base weight is 13 pounds, including a cell phone to keep my wife happy and a camera, mini-tripod, and extra battery, to keep me happy. Summer weight easily slips below 10 pounds. That's light enough.

Table of Ingredients

Item	Measure	Calories	Ounces	Calories/oz.
Almonds	1/4 c.	170.0	1.06	161
Almonds	1/3 c.	226.7	1.41	161
Apples, Dried	1/4 c.	110.0	1.41	78
Apricots, Dried	1/4 c.	110.0	1.41	78
Apricots, Dried	1/3 c.	146.7	1.88	78
Bacon Bits, Hormel Real	1 tbsp.	30.0	0.25	122
Bagel, Cinnamon & Raisin	1 bagel	250.0	3.49	72
Banana Chips	1/4 c.	150.0	1.06	142
Brown Sugar, Light	2 tbsp.	103.6	0.97	107
Brownie, store brand	1 pc	228.0	2.01	113
Bulgur with Soy	1/4 c.	115.0	1.41	82
Butter	1/4 c.	407.0	2.00	203
Butter Buds	1 tbsp.	5.0	0.07	71
Cashew halves & pieces, salted	1/4 c.	180.0	1.13	159
Cashew halves & pieces, salted	1/3 c.	240.0	1.50	159
Cheerios	1 c.	111.0	1.06	105
Cheese Danish, Kellogg's	1 pc	255.0	2.18	117
Cheese, Cheddar	1 oz.	114.0	1.00	114
Cheese, Jack	1 oz.	80.0	0.81	99
Cheese, Mozzarella	1 oz.	80.0	1.00	80
Cheese, Parmesan	1 tbsp.	12.5	0.09	142
Cheese, Swiss	1/3 c.	80.0	0.81	99
Cheesecake, No bake store brand	1/6 pkg.	220.0	1.87	118
Cherries, Dried	1/4 c.	120.0	1.41	85
Cherries, Dried	1/3 c.	160.0	1.88	85
Chicken, Sweet Sue 3 oz. foil pack	1 pkg.	100.0	2.96	34
Chocolate Chips, Semi-Sweet	1/4 c.	280.0	1.98	142
Chocolate Chips, Semi-Sweet	1/3 c.	373.3	2.63	142
Chocolate Pudding, Jell-o Instant	1/2 pkg.	200.0	1.98	101
Cinnamon	1 tsp.	6.0	0.81	7
Clams, Chicken of the Sea	1 pkg.	40.0	3.53	11
Cliff Bar, Crunchy Peanut Butter	1 bar	250.0	2.40	104

Item	Measure	Calories	Ounces	Calories/oz.
Coconut, Shredded	1/4 c.	116.5	0.82	142
Coffee, Folgers instant	2 tbsp.	2.0	0.06	32
Coffee, Folgers Singles Bag	1 bag	2.0	0.21	9
Coffee-Mate, Flavored	1 tbsp.	15.0	0.11	142
Coffee-Mate, Original	1 tbsp.	10.0	0.07	142
Corn Flour	1/4 c.	104.0	1.01	103
Couscous	1/4 c.	150.0	1.48	101
Couscous	1/3 c.	200.0	1.98	101
Crab, Chicken of the Sea	1 pkg.	40.0	3.53	11
Craisins, Cherry Flavor	1/4 c.	97.5	1.06	92
Craisins	1/3 c.	130.0	1.41	92
Cream of Wheat	1/4 c.	160.0	1.55	103
Cream of Wheat	1/3 c.	213.3	2.07	103
Dates	1 c.	502.0	6.28	80
Fig Newton	1 pc.	50.0	0.51	98
Garlic Powder	1 tsp.	9.0	0.10	91
Graham Cracker	1 sheet	70.0	0.55	128
Granola-1	1/2 c.	290.0	2.19	133
Grape Nuts	1/2 c.	200.0	2.05	98
Grits, Quaker Instant	1 pkg.	100.0	0.99	101
Harvest Bar, Toffee	1 bar	250.0	2.29	109
Honey	1/4 c.	258.0	2.99	86
Hot & Sour Soup Mix	2 tbsp.	54.0	0.55	98
Hot & Spicy Szechwan mix	2 tbsp.	15.0	0.16	95
Instant Breakfast, Regular	1 pkg.	130.0	1.27	102
Jerky, Black Pepper	1 oz.	70.0	1.00	70
Jerky, Teriyaki	1 oz.	80.0	1.00	80
Land-o-Lakes Cocoa	1 pkg.	150.0	1.23	122
M&Ms Peanut	1 bag	240.0	1.69	146
M&Ms Peanut	1/4 c.	219.0	1.50	146
M&Ms Plain	1 bag	250.0	1.74	140
M&Ms Plain	1/4 c.	256.0	1.83	140
Margarine	1/4 c.	406.0	1.99	204
Marshmallows, Tiny	1/4 c.	39.8	0.44	90
Mayo (3/4 tbsp.)	1 pkt.	42.8	0.39	110
Milk, Instant Nonfat Dry	1 tbsp.	15.0	0.15	99
Milk, Instant Nonfat Dry	1/2 c.	120.0	1.22	99

Item	Measure	Calories	Ounces	Calories/oz.
Milk, Instant Nonfat Dry	1/3 c.	80.0	0.81	99
Mushroom Gravy Mix	1 pkg.	80.0	0.74	108
Mushrooms, Shitake Dried	4 pcs.	20.0	0.20	101
Mustard (1 tsp.)	1 pkt.	3.0	0.18	17
Oil, Canola	1/4 c.	119.0	0.48	250
Oil, Olive	1 Tbsp	119.0	0.48	250
Oil, Peanut	1Tbsp	119.0	0.48	250
Oatmeal, Cinnamon & Sugar	2 pkg.	321.0	3.03	106
Oatmeal Quaker, Regular	1/2 c.	155.5	1.43	109
Onion, Flakes	1 tbsp.	17.0	0.18	96
Onion, Flakes	1/4 c.	49.0	0.49	96
Oreo	1 pc.	47.0	0.35	133
Pay Day Candy Bar	1 bar	260.0	1.83	142
Peaches, Dried	1/4 c.	96.0	1.41	68
Peaches, Dried	1/3 c.	127.0	1.88	68
Peanut Butter, Extra Crunchy	2 tbsp.	190.0	1.13	168
Peanut Butter, Smooth	2 tbsp.	200.0	1.13	177
Peanuts, Honey Roasted	1/4 c.	160.0	0.99	162
Peanuts, Honey Roasted	1/3 c.	213.3	1.32	162
Peanuts, Spanish	1/4 c.	213.0	1.30	164
Pecans, Chopped	1/4 c.	188.0	1.09	172
Pecans, Chopped	1/3 c.	251.0	1.46	172
Pepper, Black	1 tsp.	5.0	0.07	68
Pepper, Red	1 tsp.	6.0	0.06	95
Pepperoni, Hormel sliced	14 pcs.	130.0	0.99	132
Pine Nuts	1/4 c.	227.0	1.19	191
Pistachios, Kernels (49/oz.)	1 oz.	162.0	1.00	162
Pistachios, Kernels (53 /qtr. c.)	1/4 c.	176.0	1.08	162
Pita, white (6 ½" size)	1 pita	200.0	2.00	100
Pita, Whole Wheat (6 ½" size)	1 pita	170.0	2.26	75
Pop Tart, Cinnamon & Sugar	2 pcs.	438.0	3.53	124
Pop Tart, Chocolate Fudge	2 pcs.	402.0	3.67	110
Potatoes instant	1/2 c.	120.0	1.48	81
Power Bar, Peanut Butter	1 bar	240.0	2.29	105
PowerAde, Lemon-Lime	1 tbsp.	70.0	0.71	99

Item	Measure	Calories	Ounces	Calories/oz.
Pria, Caramel Nut Brownie	1 bar	170.0	1.69	100
Pudding, Instant	½ pkg.	200.0	1.83	109
Raisins	1/4 c.	123.3	1.20	103
Raisins	1/3 c.	164.0	1.60	103
Raisins, Yogurt Covered	1/4 c.	130.0	1.06	123
Raisins, Yogurt Covered	1/3 c.	173.3	1.41	123
Ramen Noodles	1 pkg.	350.0	3.03	115
Refried Beans, canned	1/2 c.	100.0	4.59	22
Rice Crispy Treat	1 pc.	190.0	2.00	95
Rice Pudding, Boxed	1/3 pk.	160.0	1.52	105
Rice, Brown instant	1/2 c.	150.0	1.52	99
Rice, White Instant	1/2 c.	160.0	1.55	103
Salt	1 tsp.	0.0	0.21	0
Sesame Seeds	1/4 c.	206.3	1.27	162
Shrimp, Foil Pack	1 pkg.	55.0	3.53	16
Slim Jim	1 pc.	50.0	0.97	52
Snickers Marathon	1 bar	220.0	1.94	113
Snickers	1 bar	280.0	2.07	135
Spaghetti Sauce Mix	1 tbsp.	25.0	0.28	89
Spaghetti Sauce Mix	1 tsp.	8.3	0.09	89
Spam, Classic	1 pkg.	210.0	3.00	70
Spam, Turkey	1 pkg.	110.0	3.00	37
Sunflower Seeds, unsalted	1/4 c.	190.0	1.06	180
Sunflower Seeds, unsalted	1/3 c.	254.7	1.46	180
Tang	2 tbsp.	90.0	0.88	102
Tea, Single Serve Bag	1 bag	2.0	0.07	28
Tomatoes, Sun Dried, Minced	1 tbsp.	40.0	0.49	81
Tortellini, Three Cheese	1/2 c.	172.5	1.48	116
Tortellini, 3 Cheese	1/3 c.	115.0	0.99	116
Tortilla, 6 inch flour	1 pc.	80.0	1.00	80
Walnuts, chopped	1 tbsp.	47.8	0.27	175
Walnuts, chopped	1/4 c.	191.0	1.09	175
Walnuts, chopped	1/3 c.	255.0	1.46	175
Weetabix, Organic	2 pcs.	120.0	1.23	97
Wheat Germ	1/4 c.	108.0	0.89	121